RRINGTON

Primary History Curriculum Guide

Primary History Curriculum Guide

PAT HUGHES, KATH COX and GILLIAN GODDARD

David Fulton Publishers
London

David Fulton Publishers Ltd
The Chiswick Centre, 414 Chiswick High Road, London W4 5TF
www.fultonpublishers.co.uk

First published in Great Britain in 2000 by David Fulton Publishers

Note: The rights of Pat Hughes, Kath Cox and Gillian Goddard to be
identified as the authors of this work have been asserted by them in accordance
with the Copyright, Designs and Patents Act 1988.

David Fulton Publishers is a division of Granada Learning Limited, part of
Granada plc.

British Library Cataloguing in Publication Data
A catalogue record for this book is available from the British Library.

ISBN 1-85346-724-3

Typeset by Elite Typesetting Techniques, Eastleigh, Hampshire
Printed and bound in Great Britain

Contents

Introduction

Aim

This guide sets out to prepare primary teacher training students to teach history well – whatever the topic or aspect of the Programme of Study. It also provides opportunities and encouragement for students to develop their own personal subject knowledge of history.

Using the book

The course content is covered in nine chapters. Each chapter begins with a statement of its learning outcomes and lists the materials that are needed to complete the work of the chapter and achieve these objectives. The chapters contain a number of tasks, some of which are optional. Although the majority of tasks can be completed at home or in a library, they will all be enriched through discussion and collaboration. Sometimes this has to be with other adults, but many tasks can also be shared with children. Space has been left within the text for readers to write in their comments and findings. Some may prefer to keep a separate history file for this. Keeping a file also means that it is possible to add additional information from other readings to build up personal resources to accompany the guide. History specialists are strongly advised to do this. Two key texts that will be needed if you wish to carry out the tasks are the National Curriculum and the History Scheme of Work. Both of these were published by DfEE/QCA in 1999 and are obtainable from QCA Publications, P.O. Box 235, Hayes, Middlesex UB3 1HF (tel: 020 8867 3333) or via the internet www.open.gov.uk/qca.

This guide can only provide a starting point to good subject knowledge and understanding of history teaching. These are skills which need constant up-dating. History may be about the past, but the way in which the past is researched, evidenced and taught changes. There are often good articles in newspapers and television programmes which show development in this area. Several newspapers include relevant websites for further information.

Focus of the course

It emphasizes the pedagogical aspects so that students learn how to teach history through focusing on:

- key historical concepts, skills and knowledge

- using historical sources

- developing a range of teaching approaches

- increasing their personal subject knowledge of history – of its methodology and of specific historical topics

- developing their own personal confidence and interest in the subject.

The course is designed to develop students' understanding of the overall requirements for primary history. It covers general principles for teaching history to pupils aged five to 11 (and the under fives). Specific content and examples reflect the emphasis of the statutory teaching requirements for the subject as set out in *The National Curriculum: Handbook for Primary Teachers in England* (DfEE/QCA 1999c; www.nc.uk.net) and *The Early Learning Goals* (DfEE/QCA 1999a; www.qca.org.uk/early-years/elg/contents.htm).

Learning outcomes

By the time the guide has been completed readers should have acquired:

- skill in identifying history as a distinctive subject with specific concepts, knowledge and skills which permeate children's lives

- knowledge of the statutory requirements for history

- knowledge of the subject matter for KS1 and/or KS2

- knowledge of the subject matter for the Foundation Stage (KS1 students and history specialists)

- teaching strategies for helping children to investigate and interpret a range of historical evidence including artefacts, oral history, visual sources, written sources, buildings and sites

- skill in identifying aspects of history which can promote their understanding of other subject areas, particularly English, information technology, geography and religious knowledge.

Chapter 1

What is History?

Learning outcomes

- What makes history different from other subjects in the primary curriculum.

- Knowledge of National Curriculum Programme of Study for Key Stages 1 and 2.

- Knowledge of the Early Learning Goals which provide a foundation for history teaching at Key Stage 1.

- Overview of the contents and organisation of the QCA schemes of work.

- Familiarity with the content of Unit 4 (KS1) and/or Unit 14 (KS2) of the QCA scheme of work.

- Skill in identifying some key historical concepts and skills.

- An exploration of some of the purposes in teaching history.

- An understanding of history as an essential element of an inclusive curriculum.

You will need

National Curriculum for History (Task 2); Newspaper (Task 4); *National Curriculum for History 1999* (Task 5); QCA Scheme of Work – Unit 4 for KS1 and Unit 14 for KS2 – access to non-fiction books on Florence Nightingale (KS1) and Ancient Greece (KS2) (Task 6).

What is history?

Since 1991, the National Curriculum has required that history be taught to all children throughout the five to 11 age-range. Prior to that, history had appeared on primary timetables in a variety of forms. Sometimes it was simply history as a distinctive timetabled subject, but often it appeared in guises such as social studies, humanities and topic work. The gradual move towards a more subject-specific curriculum is well documented in a number of texts about educational change in the last three decades of the 20th century. In the late 1980s, subject-specific working parties were set up to examine all the different curriculum areas, and their initial findings were used to inform the content of the first

National Curriculum document. The Working Party's document for history makes useful reading for history specialists (DES 1990). It identifies the purposes of history teaching and uses this rationale for recommending subject content. It is interesting to compare the latest statutory requirements for history teaching in the 21st century with the initial recommendations of the working party.

 Complete the outline below. Be honest; you may have ideas about the subject that will influence your attitude to it and your understanding of its subject essence. It is as well to identify this at an early stage. This is an interesting task to undertake with children.

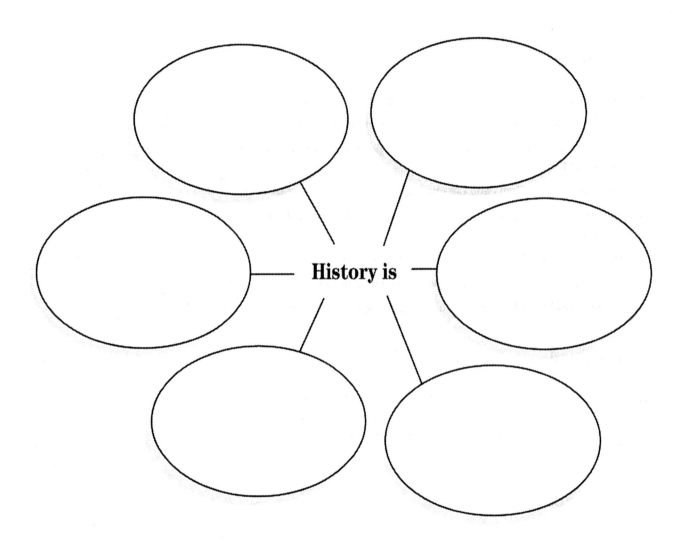

2 Compare what you have written with what is set out in the National Curriculum.

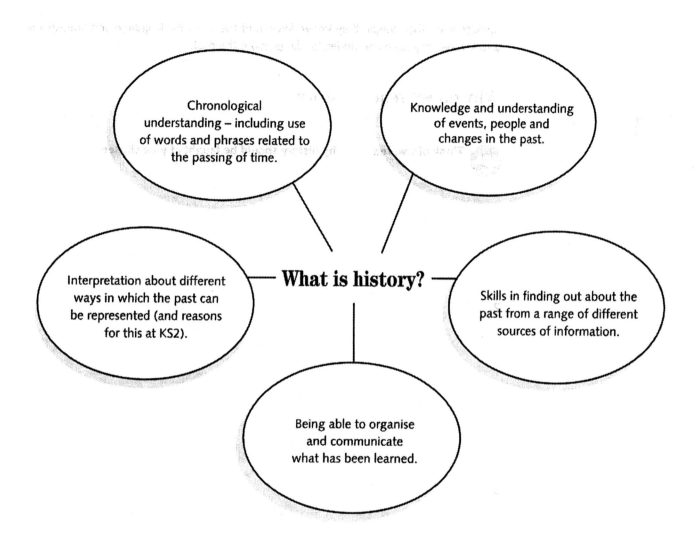

The Foundation Stage

Knowledge and understanding of the world is an area of learning for the under fives. One of the early learning goals for the end of the Foundation Stage is that pupils should be able to find out about the past and present events in their own lives and in those of their families and other people they know. Several of the goals for language and literacy will also involve language and understandings about the past.

Why do we teach history?

(3) **Think of five reasons why history should be taught at your chosen key stage.**

1.

2.

3.

4.

5.

Compare your list with someone else's before looking at the suggestions made by the National Curriculum History Working Group (following).

The National Curriculum History Working Group suggests that the purposes of school history are:

- to help understand the present in the context of the past
- to arouse interest in the past
- to help give pupils a sense of identity
- to help give pupils an understanding of their own cultural roots and shared inheritances
- to contribute to pupils' knowledge and understanding of other countries and other cultures in the modern world
- to train the mind by means of disciplined study. History relies heavily upon disciplined enquiry, systematic analysis and evaluation, argument, logical rigour and a search for truth
- to introduce pupils to the distinctive methodology of historians
- to enrich other areas of the curriculum
- to prepare pupils for adult life.

Hilary Cooper, in the third edition of her book *The Teaching of History in Primary Schools* (Cooper 2000), extends this in her two chapters on historical thinking.

You may find that you disagree with some of these purposes or that you have found additional reasons for the study of history in the primary school. However, whether we enjoyed or hated the subject when we were at school, we cannot escape from it. It is the most dangerous subject in the world because it kills!

 Look at any newspaper or television news bulletin and identify three confrontations which have their roots in different interpretations of history. They may be international, national, regional or local. Sadly it is not a difficult task.

1.

2.

3.

Historical skills

HMI identified seven objectives for pupil progress in historical skills in a document published in 1985 (*History in the Primary and Secondary Years*). These still remain a good guide to identifying specific historical skills when planning a lesson. The document is well worth seeking out because it provides a linear progression for each skill.

1. Reference and information-finding skills such as those outlined in the NLS for non-fiction texts.

2. Skills in chronology – such as the use of basic vocabulary and understanding chronology.

3. Language and historical ideas – we would probably identify these today as historical concepts such as hero, heroine, nobleman.

4. Use and analysis of evidence.

5. Empathetic understanding.

6. Asking historical questions.

7. Synthesis and communication using basic ideas.

Thinking skills and attitudes

The writers of this guide believe that history has a key role to play in encouraging children and adults to know how to think. We would be very foolish to claim that such thinking skills will create world peace, but extending the mind beyond the obvious and developing creative solutions to problems should be one outcome of good education. It is certainly a crucial element in children's social, moral, spiritual and cultural education.

Here are some pointers for creating a thinking atmosphere:

- **Examine your own thinking about thinking!** Academic skills, such as knowing how to read and memorise number facts, are not the same as thinking skills. Historical skills cover various levels of thinking – knowledge, comprehension, application, analysis, synthesis and evaluation.

- **Start early.** Under fives can be challenged to think and image. History asks them to think about the time when they were little.

- **Give children something to think about.** All historical sources provide this – museum exhibits, artefacts, portraits, photographs and so on. Challenge them to think about what they've seen and heard.

- **Teach them to look at all sides to a question/problem.** The obvious answer is not always the best one.

- **Encourage them to find threads, patterns and make connections.** How does this relate to what we did in history last week?

- **Show** how history can be seen as a dynamic force where accepted ideas are overturned.

- **Ask good and varied questions.** Knowledge-level for recalling information, unconventional questions to elicit thought 'How do you know that?'; prepare questions in advance but be prepared to follow up on the comments and understandings children have; ask questions which can be answered silently or in writing; sometimes ask pupils to repeat the question and give a good response time (3 to 5 seconds after asking the question); ask children to clarify their answers.

- **Teach children to define terms.** What is meant by the word 'old', for example? Defining terms is a tough mental discipline.

- **Encourage them to consider other points of view.** Historical fiction provides some ideas doing this.

- **Write it down.** Thoughts can be fuzzy, until clarified on paper. History can be particularly useful in clarifying formats for different types of writing – reports, recounts and explanations.

- **Encourage creativity.** Role-playing; pose 'what if?' type questions; practise divergent thinking; solve open-ended problems 'How can you make a model Tudor town house?'

- **Nurture imagination.** What would happen if a Tudor child came to visit us in school today?

People

History is about people.

 List ten people who lived at some time in the past. Sequence them (roughly) in chronological order to make a very basic timeline.

1.

2.

3.

4.

5.

6.

7.

8.

9.

10.

Now ask yourself these questions:

- **What type of people are they?**

- **Why are they remembered?**

- **What aspects of human endeavour do they represent?**

- **Are there any women on your list?**

- **Do any represent different cultures?**

- **Have you included any members of your family? If not, do so.**

Add yourself to the timeline.

Add the name of one of the children you have taught.

School history has been criticised as being exclusive because the subject matter concentrates on Eurocentric, wealthy males. In *Reclaiming Our Pasts*, Claire (1996) argues strongly for a more inclusive history curriculum for the primary school:

- children need to contextualise the information they are getting through the media in order to understand it better

- they are interested anyway

- a Eurocentric and male-centred curriculum fails to prepare children adequately for life

- a Eurocentric and male-centred curriculum is basically unjust and biased about the contributions and history of women and non-European people

- this limited curriculum continues to support sexism, racism and class misunderstanding by perpetuating out-dated attitudes.

She points out that this is not just about trendy 'political correctness' but is central to a number of subject related issues. These include:

- The relationship between British history and world history – this is a crucial part of historical interpretation. The National Curriculum at KS2 extends the need to identify different ways in which the past is represented and interpreted to giving reasons for this.

- The need to avoid teaching pupils a version of history which sees history as a 'march of progress', where political, social and economic aspects of life get progressively better. The great 19th century historians spent little time on the failures and the experience of the marginalised or less fortunate groups such as the colonised or poor. Today, politicians speak of their own great changes and frequently forget particular aspects of the recent past which may have been more supportive to the majority of people.

- The need to encourage children to find out about the histories of their own communities and draw on this to avoid an imperialist, Eurocentric and male-centred view of the world. The movements of people is a fascinating subject in itself. Nursery children may have moved themselves or know people who have moved. The local community may include a number of communities with varied heritages and languages. All of the studies at KS2 involve movements of peoples – the Romans, Anglo-Saxons and Vikings; Tudor exploration; movements of peoples into the cities in Victorian times and immigration and emigration in Britain since 1930.

Primary school history has to take account of 'race' and ethnicity, gender and class. Local publications are often very good at doing this and the history channel on the television often reflects this broader approach to history, as do many of the websites linked to these programmes (e.g. www.thehistorychannel.co.uk/). Unfortunately pupils still meet traditional and biased historical accounts in other subject areas. Some of the materials used in English lessons are rooted in history, but the subject content is ignored and children are asked to read and write with little insight into the context.

 Read through the programme of study for history in the National Curriculum for either KS1 or KS2. Identify the five different elements involved. Continue to read the relevant section on the breadth of study. You might find it useful to draw these up into a table.

Title	Key Stage 1	Key Stage 2
1. Chronology	Pupils should be taught	Pupils should be taught
2.	Pupils should be taught	Pupils should be taught
3.	Pupils should be taught	Pupils should be taught
4.	Pupils should be taught	Pupils should be taught
5.	Pupils should be taught	Pupils should be taught

Key historical concepts

A concept is an abstract notion related to an idea. As we grow older, our understanding of concepts develops and changes. For example, a young child may start to identify the 'concept' or idea of a dog as compared to the 'concept' or idea of a cat. Later, the child may be able to distinguish between different types of dog, later still the child as a dog-owner may find out much more about the particular breed of dog. A concept is more than a single word, although being able to read and use the word in its correct context is a starting point for discussion about the concept. Key concepts in history are chronology, change, continuity, cause and effect. Concepts such as change and continuity, cause and effect are closely linked. Cooper (2000) explores historical concepts in relation to psychologists' research into the development of concepts. She also gives examples of work carried out by student teachers investigating concepts of time.

Chronology

 (Optional) Making a timeline: Chronology is a key concept in history. Children can be encouraged to begin to extend their understanding of chronology through sequencing activities using a simple timeline. A basic timeline provides a valuable resource which can be adapted through the use of different labels to promote chronological understanding at different levels. A timeline is an essential resource in a primary classroom.

KS1 – Devise a timeline for yourself which records the changes in your own life. Your own timeline is also useful for teaching aspects of local history at KS2 and Britain Since 1930.

KS2 – Devise a timeline for one of the British history studies. It is useful to consult two or three timelines for the same period and note inclusions and omissions.

Personal Timeline – Children are fascinated by their teachers' lives. This was evident in children's responses to the following examples. Sharon presented KS1 children with a timeline composed of photographs of herself from birth to 30. She scanned in the photographs and put a date under each one. The timeline was then laminated and spread out down the corridor. It showed changes in her life – birth, birthdays, graduation, marriage, children. It also showed changes in fashion, transport and leisure activities. Some of these were related to age, but many were related to historical changes in her lifetime. Colin, another KS1 student, included a series of artefacts on his timeline – a birthday card, a swimming certificate, the key to his first flat and a business card to show that he once worked as an insurance agent. Both the timelines were large and bold, so that children could gain some understanding of the expanse of time.

Serial Timeline – If selected carefully, old and dated textbooks are a good source of illustrative material for KS2 timelines. A 1970s secondary history book may be no use for primary children, but may have some good illustrations which can be used on a timeline. Many museums and historical sites sell postcards showing reconstructions, in addition to photographs of artefacts and sections of old buildings. Many websites have good colour photographs and illustrations. The National Portrait Gallery (on www.npg.org.uk/roomsg.htm) and the National Gallery (on www.nationalgallery.org.uk/collection/content.html) are particularly useful. Try to avoid stereotyped historical graphics, which appear on some of the less professional websites. A timeline of the Roman invasion and settlement in Britain could show key dates and events, illustrated by a postcard of someone dressed up as a Roman soldier, pictures of reconstructed Roman villas and towns and postcards of some of the artefacts which have been found at sites of settlements.

Pat Hoodless (1996) in *Time and Timelines in the Primary School* looks at this in more detail, but most texts on the teaching of primary history have sections which focus on chronology and timelines.

Other key historical concepts

Historians identify several concepts which they see as being key elements of history. Here are a number of them which children will meet before they finish in primary school. Can you think of any more? Which concepts will children meet at the Foundation Stage? If you look at one of the themes for Key Stage 2, such as Ancient Greece, you could tick some of the concepts which children are likely to meet when they study that.

AD/BC	administration	anachronism
ancient	archaeology	aristocratic
authority	bias	bishop
cause	change	civilisation
classical	colony/colonialism	conclusion
continuity	democratic	development
economic	empire	evidence
frontier	government	hero/heroine
industrial	king/queen	law
legal	modern	monarchy
myth	nation	old
oligarchy	parliament	past
political	power	primary source
progress	propaganda	protestant
secondary source	social	society
religion	war	welfare state

Changing meanings

Many concepts have different meanings in different contexts. The word 'change', for example, can be used in history to describe changes caused by the passing of time. For instance, we may look at a photograph of the beach at Blackpool at the start of the 20th century and make comparisons with a picture of the same beach today. If children are asked to describe 'the historical changes' they need to be clear about what is a historical change.

A mixed class of Y2s and Y3s were asked what they thought of when someone said the word 'change'. Here are some of their replies.

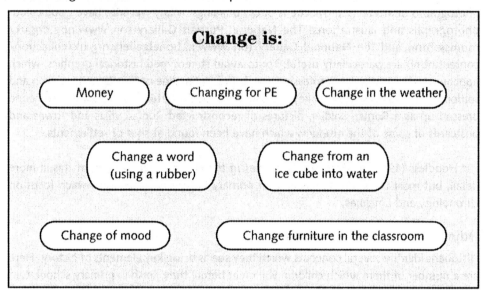

Change is:

Money   Changing for PE   Change in the weather

Change a word (using a rubber)   Change from an ice cube into water

Change of mood   Change furniture in the classroom

Concepts linked to words such as 'new' and 'old' are often worth exploring with young children. 'Old' may be interpreted as broken, old-fashioned, useless, ready to throw out such as an old toy. 'Old' used as an adjective to describe a human being could be misinterpreted in the same way. Valuable antiques are a good way of looking at 'old' in a more positive light, also 'old' as favourite as in an 'old' teddy bear.

Historical concepts as word-level work in literacy

A surprising amount of history comes into word-level work in the Literacy Strategy at both key stages.

Many commonly-used words and phrases draw on complex historical concepts which may be difficult for children to understand if they have little understanding of history. For instance:

1. Words that relate to the passing of time which require readers and writers to have an understanding of chronology. This group includes commonly-used words and phrases such as 'ancient', 'after', 'a long time ago', 'before', 'century', 'decade', 'millennium', 'modern', 'past', 'present'. Many of these are temporal connectives and are an important part of 'the history register' in informational texts. They link one part of a sentence or paragraph to another. Weak readers often can read the words but then have difficulty making sense of the whole passage because they have failed to comprehend the relationship between one part of the sentence/paragraph and the other. Bobbie Neate (1999) goes into this in more detail in her book *Finding Out About Finding Out*.

2. Period specific words and phrases to denote a particular period of time, for example 'the Victorian era', 'the Viking period'.

3. Words such as 'Empire', which can be linked to period words – 'The Roman Empire', 'the Victorian Empire'.

4. Words that are period specific, such as words associated with Tudor houses, for example 'long gallery', 'buttery' and 'inventory'.

5. Words that have gone from common usage, but are found in traditional rhymes and jingles – 'muffin man', 'halfpenny', 'crown' (as in Jack and Jill), 'curds and whey'.

6. Words that are historical concepts related to specific groups of people – 'settlers', 'kings', 'Romans', 'invaders'.

7. Phrases that have specific meanings, for example 'the area we know now as...'

8. Etymology –

   • evolution of words for food and drink, e.g. pizza and pasta from Italy

   • topographical elements in place names

   • street names

   • personal names

   • surnames

   • eponymous words – teddy bear (Theodore Roosevelt)

   • eponymous places – marathon (Marathon, Greece)

   • eponymous people – atlas (Greek Titan, Atlas)

   • lexical invasions – social (Latin); silver (Norse)

   • ancient mutations – goose/geese (Old English).

There are several 'Big Books' on the market such as those in the Heinemann *Literacy Worlds* series and Longman's *Pelican* series which can be used to support lexical history in the Literacy Hour.

Schemes of Work

The Qualifications and Curriculum Authority (QCA) and the Standards and Effectiveness Unit of the Department of Education and Employment produced a Scheme of Work for history in 1998. This was updated in 2000 to take heed of Curriculum 2000. This drew on the work devised by teachers and schools since the implementation of the National Curriculum History programmes in 1991. The Scheme of Work is not statutory, but provides some useful guidelines for non-specialist teachers of the subject. As with all schemes of work, the scheme should be adapted for the specific needs of the school and, like the geography Scheme of Work, it needs to take account of specific cultural groups within the community as well as maximising the opportunities provided by the local area.

Units 1 to 5 cover Key Stage 1 and units 6A to 16 cover Key Stage 2. Each unit represents a medium-term plan, covering a term or less.

Year Group	Unit Number	Unit Title
1	1	How are our toys different from those in the past?
2	2	What were homes like a long time ago?
1 or 2	3	What were seaside holidays like in the past?
2	4	Why do we remember Florence Nightingale?
2	5	How do we know about the Great Fire of London?
3 or 4	6A	Why have people invaded and settled in Britain in the past? A Roman case study.
3 or 4	6B	Why have people invaded and settled in Britain in the past? An Anglo-Saxon case study.
3 or 4	6C	Why have people invaded and settled in Britain in the past? A Viking case study.
3 or 4	7	Why did Henry VIII marry six times?
3 or 4	8	What were the differences between the lives of the rich and poor people in Tudor times?
3 or 4	9	What was it like for children in the Second World War?
3 or 4	10	What can we find out about ancient Egypt from what has survived?
5 or 6	11	What was it like for children living in Victorian Britain?
5 or 6	12	How did life change in our locality in Victorian times?
5 or 6	13	How has life in Britain changed since 1948?
5 or 6	14	Who were the ancient Greeks?
5 or 6	15	How do we use ancient Greek ideas today?
5 or 6	16	How can we find out about the Indus Valley civilisation?

Four additional units were produced for the 2000 update

Unit Number	Unit Title
17	What are we remembering on Remembrance Day? (year 2)
18	What was it like to live here in the past? (years 3/4)
19	What were the effects of Tudor exploration? (years 5/6)
20	What can we learn about recent history from studying the life of a famous person? (years 5/6)

Borrow the history QCA Scheme of Work from a school or library, or download from the Internet on www.open.gov.uk/qca.

1. Look at Unit 4 (KS1) and/or Unit 14 (KS2).

2. Identify the 10 or 11 different headings into which it is divided.

3. Find a number of adult or child textbooks which can provide you with more information about this particular unit.

4. Choose one teaching subsection e.g. Who was Florence Nightingale? (Unit 4) or What do the sources tell us about the importance of the Olympic games to the ancient Greeks? (Unit 14)

5. Identify some resources you would need to teach this subsection effectively.

Good history teaching is very resource heavy. Teaching historical knowledge, skills and understanding involves children using a wide range of sources of information; for example, documents, printed sources, photographs, artefacts, historic buildings, galleries and sites. ICT websites give access to an increasing number of these sources. Most schools have very good resource boxes for history and many LEAs, museums and libraries lend materials to support effective teaching. Several of the following sections explore ways in which these resources can be used most effectively. There are obvious parallels with the use of resources for other subjects such as artefacts and buildings in religious education and photographs in geography.

Chapter 2

Planning, Teaching and Assessing Historical Knowledge, Skills and Understanding

Learning outcomes

- To examine own understanding of history in relation to planning, teaching and assessing.

- To develop knowledge and skills in planning history.

- To recognise the necessity to use a variety of teaching methods to ensure effective teaching of the subject.

- To be familiar with ways in which history is assessed.

- To become familiar with the content of Unit 2 (KS1) or Unit 6A (KS2) of the QCA Scheme of Work.

You will need

National Curriculum Document History (1999) www.nc.uk.net (for Task 1); QCA Unit 2 (KS1) or Unit 6A (KS2) www.open.gov.uk/qca/ (for Task 2)

National Curriculum 1999

In history, pupils find evidence, weigh it up and reach their own conclusion. To do this they need to be able to research, sift through evidence, and argue for their point of view – skills that are prized in adult life. The National Curriculum Handbook *(1999c)*

History is an unusual discipline. Its core is hard fact that you cannot get away from and have to learn to master. At the same time you have to be deductive, perceptive and imaginative in the use of that fact. The National Curriculum Handbook *(1999c)*

This view of history as an investigative activity may not be how you remember your own school history. One of the authors of this guide remembers very strongly doing nothing but taking notes for her A level history. The only 'skill' involved was learning how to remember them. Fortunately, school history has moved on from that but the skills required need to be planned, taught and assessed. If you retain a view of history as a series of facts to be learned, then your planning and teaching will reflect this and assessment becomes memory testing. The trivial pursuits approach to history is ineffective in delivering the statutory requirements – although quizzes can be incorporated into your teaching strategies. If you are concerned about your subject knowledge there are several excellent books and websites available. Make a start with the relevant resource packs available in school. Cooper (2000) is particularly good for subject specialists who plan to become subject managers.

 Re-examine what you wrote in Unit 1 about 'What is history?'. Ask yourself again how this compared with what the National Curriculum Document states and with the above two introductory statements taken from the general introduction to the Programmes of Study (page 103).

Most schools have good long- and medium-term plans for history and even when the statutory requirements have changed they have been adapted easily to fit in with new requirements. Many schools do more than the basic minimum by:

- building on firm foundations for the subject established at the Foundation Stage in the nursery and reception class

- using story and assembly time for stories about famous people and events

- adopting a longitudinal approach to local history and geography, so that pupils revisit, consolidate and extend their knowledge of their local community throughout their primary schooling. This means they do more than one local history unit and build up important skills in using a variety of local historical sources

- building on historical fiction and non-fiction used in the Literacy Hour

- combining historical context with extended English writing sessions

- using historical based CD-ROMs and websites in timetabled ICT time

- having timelines and history displays around the school so that different aspects of the subject permeate children's school environment

- linking history with 'new' areas of the curriculum such as PSHE (Personal, Social and Health Education) and citizenship (see *History Teachers Guide Update*, QCA 2000, page 7)

- drawing on historical content when taking children out of school – geography locality studies, trips to museums, art galleries and so on

- drawing on historical content for trips inside school, for example familiarising new pupils with the school layout

- studying one British theme unit such as the Victorians and then linking the alternative, Britain Since 1930, with the local study unit

- giving children history homework to encourage research skills – this is often surprisingly popular with parents as more than one OFSTED report shows.

QCA planning guidance

Long-term planning

This is outlined under Schemes of Work towards the end of the previous chapter of this guide.

Medium-term planning

These are separate unit titles within the Scheme of Work. Individual units can be downloaded from www.open.gov.uk/qca/

Short-term planning

Schools vary in their approach to short-term planning. Student teachers, however, are expected to have detailed short-term plans with a lesson or activity plan for every historical activity. This includes on-going small group activities. For example, at Key Stage 1, if the home corner is turned into a living room from a long time ago, there need to be specific learning objectives, structured teaching activities and identifiable means of assessing children's learning. At Key Stage 2, children may be asked to research into mummification as part of their history homework on ancient Egypt. This also needs specific learning objectives so that children and their parents are clear about what is expected.

Short-term planning becomes much more difficult when the focus is on another subject area such as English, where the learning objectives in the short-term planning are English. As students become more confident, cross-curricular links become more obvious and short-term planning for history taught within other subject areas can be identified within the history medium-term plans and recorded as background information in the history short-term plans.

Planning structure: the key questions approach

Both the QCA long- and medium-term planning follow a long tradition of using key questions to give a focus to history-based work. This approach can also be found in many commercial schemes as well as in the school and LEA schemes. All of the QCA Unit Titles are posed as questions, for example: *What were homes like a long time ago?* (Unit 2, Y1) and *Why have people invaded and settled in Britain in the past?* (Units 6A/B/C).

In the medium-term planning, this is followed up by more specific questions such as:

Unit 2: What were homes like a long time ago?	Unit 6A: Why have people invaded and settled in Britain in the past? [A Roman case study]
What sort of homes do people live in today?	Why do people move away from where they were born?
What can we find out from the outside of homes?	Who invaded and settled in Britain a long time ago?
How were homes long ago different from homes today?	Who were the Celts and who were the Romans? Who was Boudicca?
What would we find inside people's homes a long time ago?	What happened in AD60?
What can we find out about Victorian or Edwardian times from looking at household objects?	What were the short-term and long-term results of Boudicca's revolt?
How can we turn the 'home corner' into a bathroom, kitchen or living room from a long time ago?	How did the Romans change Britain when they settled here?

This key questions approach has a long research base dating from the 1960's and 1970's Schools Council work on humanities. In fact historians reading this will recognise a teaching strategy dating back to Ancient Greece, where philosophers explored ideas with their students on a question and answer basis. More recently it has been outlined in the First Steps Project Work on Literacy (First Steps 1997) and David Wray and Maureen Lewis's work for the National Literacy Strategy (Module 6: Using Non-fiction) and their book *Developing Children's Non-fiction Writing* (Lewis and Wray 1995). This suggests effective teaching of learning skills is done through a three way process known as *KWL*. That is:

- What do we know (K), i.e. prior learning

- What do we want to know (W), i.e. questions for research

- What have we learnt (L), i.e. record our knowledge.

It has been recognised that children may not ask the questions that we need them to ask in order to make progress in their learning, so the history planning scheme supplies the questions for them! This does have problems, but the skilful teacher can generally persuade pupils to ask the questions for which s/he had planned.

Teaching strategies for teaching questioning

Teaching children to ask relevant questions is an important strategy. We brainstorm what we already know (K) about the Romans (KS2) or Homes long ago (KS1). We can cheat here by helping pupils with a display of books, poster or an initial story. This gives them a feeling that they 'know something', even if it is limited to recognising a picture and a title on a book. The next stage moves children on to asking '*What do we want to know about homes long ago/The Romans?*' *What sort of words will start our questions? What punctuation will finish them? What? When? Where? Which? Who? How?* etc. Older pupils move on to more complex questions, but this strategy produces a simple structure to raise pertinent questions.

Homes	The Romans
What sort of homes do people live in today?	When did they come to Britain?
What can we find out from the outside of homes?	What did they do?
How were homes long ago different from homes today?	Why do we learn about them?

Teaching strategies for skills-based learning

The National Curriculum for history identifies several different skills which pupils are expected to acquire and develop as a result of following the Programmes of Study. Most of the skills are cross-curricular, but history offers more opportunities than many subjects for children to explore and develop these key life skills. It is humbling to remind ourselves that most of this skills-learning starts at birth, and that teachers have a tremendous responsibility to plan for their continued development within the school setting. Skills include:

1. Chronological understanding
- placing events and objects into chronological order
- using the appropriate vocabulary
- understanding ourselves and our place in time
- understanding others and their place in time

2. Interpreting different ways in which the past is represented
- recalling and recounting the same type of information from different sources
- investigating
- comparing and contrasting
- looking for bias (both in the past and present)
- problem solving

3. Enquiry
- questioning
- hypothesising
- planning investigations
- researching – finding, collecting and recording information
- information handling
- study skills, including a wide variety of different non-fiction genres from different periods in time

4. Organising and communicating
- discussion and debate with one another/carers and friends as well as with the teacher
- writing – narrative and a variety of non-fiction genres, such as descriptions, recounts, explanations, procedural texts and discussion
- presenting findings to the class as displays, exhibitions, models, photographs and illustrations, drama, audio-visual, graphs, maps, charts
- evaluating their own work.

Investigating teaching strategies

 Identifying the specific skills required to teach the history Programme of Study helps to focus on possible teaching activities. Look through the possible teaching activities for Unit 2 'What were homes like a long time ago?' (KS1) or Unit 6A 'Why have people invaded and settled in Britain in the past? A Roman case study' (KS2), and make your own list.

You may have included:

- presentations – by the teacher, by other adults, by older children, by children themselves

- focused teaching for use of source material

- discussion and debate

- question and answer

- individual and group investigations using a wide variety of different source material, including visual and written sources and artefacts

- television, radio, tape, video, film, ICT

- role-play and drama

- field work, visits to museums and historic sites.

The need for variety in teaching strategies is clear from the teaching objectives. It is these which provide the crucial impetus for effective teaching and learning. Clear learning objectives focus teaching, so that pupils' learning is effective and can be recorded.

Short-term planning: the lesson plan

1. Objectives

- Aim for no more than three history focused learning objectives.

- Include a knowledge-based objective and a skills-based one.

- Make them precise, so that at the end of the lesson you can assess whether your teaching has been effective and exactly what children have learned as a result of it.

2. Content

- Build on children's prior knowledge – you cannot claim effective teaching has taken place if pupils had already consolidated the knowledge and skills covered by the lesson.

- Demonstrate varied teaching strategies over a sequence of lessons.

- Vary organisational formats so that history does not always replicate the format of the literacy and numeracy lessons.

- Time the format to avoid overlong teacher presentations – pupils' listening skills may improve but at the expense of other vital skills!

- Demonstrate good subject knowledge.

Creating a lesson plan or sequence of lesson plans for history will involve adapting any exemplar scheme of work. School and commercially-based schemes are written for experienced teachers so both NQT and student teachers will need to work hard to make their own. QCA Schemes of Work will need to be modified for meeting the needs of the children in any particular school and maximising the opportunities provided by the local area. You may wish to consider the extent to which:

- the QCA unit or the commercially-based scheme is written for a different year group from the one you are teaching

- features of the local area can be used to enhance your scheme (museums, sites)

- children's own experience can be identified and then built on

- the school resources history and whether there are alternative resources that can be used (library loans, museum loans, own evidence collections, presentation from a friend)

- the material in an existing scheme will need to be adapted for specific children – lower and higher attaining children

- planning and teaching can be differentiated for mixed aged classes which are studying the same topic.

Assessment

The QCA Schemes of Work take a pragmatic view of assessment in history. The writers point out that their learning outcomes show how children can demonstrate what they have learned. They then suggest that this work will serve as a record for classes working on each unit and **it is not necessary to make detailed records for each child in relation to these outcomes.**

This acknowledges what most schools were already doing prior to the introduction of the QCA scheme. Assessments include:

1. Assessment by content coverage. Children are assumed to have reached the learning outcomes if they have attended the lesson and completed any task set. This is probably by far the most common method of assessing history because it is so easy to manage.

2. Assessment by attainment levels. The simplest form of doing this uses a checklist approach linked to the attainment levels for history. So, for Level 1 a class checklist would read as shown on the chart below.

3. Assessment through a more detailed breakdown of knowledge and skills. Lesson objectives are written in this format and assessment is made for individual children on the basis of whether these objectives have been achieved. There is much to be said for breaking this down into a record of the 'Wow's' and the 'Ough's' of the lesson, i.e. recording the surprises and disappointments of individual learning.

	Name of child													
Can recognise distinction between past and present in own and other people's lives.														
Shows emerging sense of chronology by placing a few events in order.														
Uses everyday chronological terms: before, after, a long time ago.														
Knows and recounts some stories from the past.														
Can find answers to simple questions using photographs, pictures, certificates and artefacts.														

Target setting

QCA guidance includes end of unit expectations which provide broad descriptions of achievement within each unit. This allows teachers to decide whether a child's progress differs markedly from that of the rest of the class. Planning needs to be adapted if there is a systematic mismatch.

Many of the cross-curricular skills used in history are key for pupil's academic development. Children who are under-achieving need to be identified and specific objectives set for them. It is also worth noting those children who have difficulty concentrating in the Literacy Hour but are willing to spend hours at home and at school going through non-fiction texts about the ancient Egyptians and feeding you interesting little titbits from their research. A positive response to many history topics can encourage motivation in the basic subjects.

Auditing the promotion of positive attitudes

The following table may be used to audit the promotion of positive attitudes; these objectives could also be used in planning.

Positive attitudes	Evidence within the key stage/year/topic	Action points
Enjoying learning • show enjoyment and enthusiasm for history • express an interest in history • show curiosity about the world • show curiosity about the history covered presently within curriculum • exhibit the desire to find out more		
Gaining confidence through learning • develop confidence to use or apply knowledge and understanding gained in history • use of resources to find out more • concentrate on and persevere to completion of task • enter sensibly into role-play situations		
Appreciating new ideas • be open-minded about learning • not always having to be right • be interested in and prepared to consider the views of an opposing side • begin to appreciate the pros and cons of a situation • explore moral dilemmas • discuss a balanced viewpoint • develop an understanding and respect for others		
The wider application of knowledge • be objective and critical of own work • develop an awareness of the complexity of some aspects of history • appreciate the role history plays in shaping our lives • appreciate that beliefs and values may have been different in the past		

Chapter 3

Evidence

Learning outcomes

- To understand what is meant by historical 'evidence'.
- To know which skills are needed to analyse historical evidence.
- To be aware of some of the problems associated with historical evidence.
- To be able to plan activities which develop children's skills of analysis.

You will need

- Handbag, briefcase or satchel including contents (for Task 1)
- Evidence collection – occupational (for KS1); personal collection of someone aged 60+ (for KS2).

What is evidence?

Nearly every day of our lives we are asked to provide some form of evidence. Often it is electronic, a security password to get into a computer or cash point. But often it is paper based. Think of the evidence you were required to provide to undertake a degree course. Certificates continue to provide evidence throughout our lives. An essential part of professional development involves adding to the initial certificates.

Evidence is a key historical concept: the 'raw materials' of history. It is through examining the available source material (evidence) for a particular period in the past that historians are able to re-construct a picture of life at that time. All pupils should be introduced to, and have the opportunity to work with, a variety of appropriate evidence in order to understand that the evidence of the past comes in many forms. Sometimes the idea of examining historical evidence is seen as something done by older children, but it is important for all children, whatever their age, to see, touch and smell items from the past. Three-year-olds who visits an historic house may spend less time there than ten-year-olds, but will still extend their experience. Many years ago, one of the authors of this guide took a photograph of her two under-fives outside Speke Hall in Liverpool. Years later, the children would look through the photo album and comment on remembering the visit. Some museums are particularly good at working with and for the very young. www.24hourmuseum.org.uk provides detailed information about facilities at local museums.

The following section outlines some of the more traditional forms of historical evidence: evidence which tells us about the past. You may be able to think of some additional ones. Certainly, developments in technology have lead to additional evidence being found to tell us more about the past.

Historical sources for under fives, KS1 and KS2

Children should have opportunities to learn about the past from a range of historical sources, such as:

ARTEFACTS Survivals from the past, such as tools, pottery, ornaments, statues, coins, carvings, tiles and fragments. Museums provide the most accessible opportunities for children to view artefacts from the more distant past.

BUILDINGS Local buildings, historic houses, sites, reconstructions, ruins, the countryside (roads, fields and placenames).

MUSIC Original recordings, recreated music, songs, radio programmes.

ADULTS Family, local history groups, age reminiscence groups.

WRITTEN

- Printed evidence such as certificates, newspapers, magazines, non-fiction texts, autobiographies, biographies, documents, letters, posters, handbills, maps, plays, stories, statistics.

- Hand-written evidence such as letters, logbooks, legal records, carved inscriptions, diaries, memoirs, scrolls, inventories, church records (births, deaths and marriages).

VISUAL SOURCES Photographs, paintings, portraits, drawings, videotapes, film.

ICT CD-ROMs, databases, virtual tours of museums and sites.

Many of these sources can come fairly cheaply from families, school resource boxes, museum loans, library loans, museum shops, car boot sales and flea markets. Others can be purchased from catalogues of firms specialising in supplying such materials for schools. Several of these firms also produce teachers' notes indicating different ways in which the evidence can be used.

Historical evidence can be divided into two categories:

1. Primary evidence

This is when the evidence or sources come from the time that is being investigated; for example a 1900's photograph of a street at the time, a Victorian button hook, an adult talking about their 1950's childhood and a Greek vase in a museum.

2. Secondary evidence

This is when the evidence or sources are produced at a later date but are based on primary source material; for example an illustration of a street at the turn of the century, a replica Victorian button hook, a modern television programme for children that is set in the 1950s and a replica Greek lamp.

The availability of the evidence varies according to the period under consideration. For example, a topic focusing on Britain since the 1930s will offer a wider range of primary source material than one in which the pupils investigate life in ancient Greece. Furthermore some forms of evidence are more accessible to younger pupils or pupils with reading difficulties – artefacts, people and visual sources.

 Take eight items of your own from a bag or brief case or child's satchel. Write down the items, i.e. make an inventory. (i) What would a stranger know about you or the child from these items? (ii) What would a stranger be able to deduce from the items? (iii) How could they find out more? (iv) How could they find out if they were right? (v) List the skills you used to enquire and interpret the evidence.

1.   5.

2.   6.

3.   7.

4.   8.

(i)

(ii)

(iii)

(iv)

(v)

Evidence skills

Children need a structured approach in order to develop the skills that will enable them to extract information from historical evidence/sources. These skills will be used to interpret any form of evidence.

- **Observation** Handling an object and often touching, looking, smelling and even listening.

- **Discussion** Describing the features of an artefact/building; identifying details in a picture.

- **Analysis** Asking questions such as 'What do you think this might be?', 'What kind of person might have used it?', 'What do you think is the story of this painting?', 'What do you think is happening in the photograph?' and 'Why might this person say that?'. It is important to model open questions to children so that they in turn learn to ask open questions themselves. History provides an opportunity for children to show curiosity about new and different experiences, rather than be fearful of something different and strange. Open questions support this approach.

- **Hypothesising** Possibilities are suggested, such as 'It could be used for...', 'It might be a...', 'The people in the photograph might have been...' and 'The lady in the painting may have wanted...'. Looking at evidence opens up opportunities for exploring doubts. As so often in life, there may be no 'right' answer.

- **Justifying** Children give reasons for their interpretation through answering questions such as 'How do you know?', 'What makes you think that?' and 'Why do you say that?'

- **Research** Can children find out more? Can they suggest ways in which they might do this? This might include: asking the person concerned, looking in a book, visiting a museum or asking an Internet question line such as 'Ask Jeeves'.

It is obvious that these skills are not confined to history but are relevant to other curriculum areas. They can be developed with the youngest pupils as with those at the end of the primary school. Initially, it is helpful to introduce the idea of evidence through non-historical activities which use familiar contexts.

Evidence bags

One of the best ways of developing evidence skills is through the use of an evidence bag. This was first introduced in the Place and Time project of the mid 1970s. The basic idea behind the activity is that children investigate a collection of 'clues' or evidence and suggest an interpretation. This activity can be adapted to suit any level from Nursery to adult. There follows a number of examples that could be incorporated into a topic for under fives and Key Stage 1 children or used as an introductory activity with Key Stage 2 pupils to get them thinking.

Evidence bags are also useful for adult helpers working with small groups of children who have difficulty expressing their thoughts. A simple bag, such as the first one 'Getting to Know You', allows children to name and describe simple objects. They can then hypothesise about the context for the objects and listen and comment to others' responses. In these circumstances, it is often a relief for children to discover that there is no one right answer and that several answers can be accepted. This helps to give children self-esteem and provides a meaningful literacy activity for adults working with small groups. The adult must be well briefed to understand the purposes of the task, so that it does not become a closed activity, with children searching for the 'one' right answer.

Examples of evidence collections

1. Ourselves
- teacher's bag 'Getting to Know You'

- child's bag of clues

- collections for different ages (baby/five-year-old)

2. Families
- generation bag (mixed)

- individual person

- lost bag/purse/wallet

- family dustbin bag

- grocery shopping bag

3. Holidays
- lost suitcase

- what did I do on my holiday? (travel tickets, souvenirs etc.)

4. Celebrations
- birthday bag for different ages (baby/10-year-old)

- mixed celebration bag (child)

- mixed celebrations (adult)

- festival bag (Christmas, Divali etc.)

5. Food
- kitchen bin bag 'What do I eat for breakfast?'

- child's lunch bag (wrappings, peel etc.)

6. Work/people who help us
- occupation bag (post person/nurse/mechanic/plumber)

7. Collections of evidence from the near past
- old suitcase or bag with photographs/documents/artefacts from a member of your family.

These activities offer a way of introducing pupils to the fact that artefacts/visual materials/ written evidence can give information. They begin to reason and be aware of some of the problems concerning evidence such as 'red herrings', ambiguous items, incomplete pictures. Beginning with a familiar context develops confidence and enables pupils to draw on existing knowledge and prior experience of the world to make interpretations. The skills are then more easily transferred to historical evidence.

 Create an evidence collection. This should be either an occupation bag (KS1) or a collection from someone who is 60+, i.e. who has lived through WW2 (KS2). Find someone to swap collections and then work through each other's collections. See if you can make a story about the person from the evidence collection you have. You may include 'a red herring' if the collection looks very easy to analyse. Record:

1. The details of your collection, i.e. the inventory

2. The details of your colleague's collection

3. Ways in which you could assess children's responses to this activity

Inclusive curriculum

In mono-cultural schools there is a need to move on from evidence bags collected by children and adults connected to the school. Children need to explore and celebrate other cultures and heritages. Use your course contacts initially to build up other forms of evidence bags to widen children's experiences. This can be particularly fruitful if linked to e-mail or snail mail contacts in other areas of the country/world.

Assessment, recording and target setting

This will be carried out mainly by listening to children's oral responses and recording can take a pictorial or written form. All the activities below can be linked to different levels of attainment in the National Curriculum Document (1999b). Children's actual responses need to be noted to identify (or evidence!) which level they have reached. A lively discussion with a group of Y6 pupils on an evidence collection from WW2 could easily produce several good examples of pupils' levels of attainment.

- Can children observe and describe the evidence?

- If relevant can they place the evidence collection in any sort of chronological order?

- Can they recognise the distinction between their own life and the story the evidence collection tells?

- Can the child move from description to reasoning?

- Is an interpretation offered?

- Is the justification logical/sensible?

- Can the child explain the reason for his/her interpretation?

- Has the child made connections with existing knowledge and experience in reaching a conclusion?

- Can he/she offer different interpretations?

- Can he/she explain why it may not be possible to be certain?

- Is the child able to suggest how he/she could find out more?

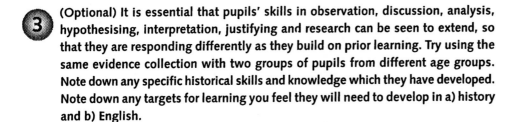 **(Optional) It is essential that pupils' skills in observation, discussion, analysis, hypothesising, interpretation, justifying and research can be seen to extend, so that they are responding differently as they build on prior learning. Try using the same evidence collection with two groups of pupils from different age groups. Note down any specific historical skills and knowledge which they have developed. Note down any targets for learning you feel they will need to develop in a) history and b) English.**

a.

b.

Evidence: photocopiable sheets and a word of warning

There are many photocopiable sheets on the market which replicate this evidence activity. Indeed, the authors of this guide have produced several themselves! They need to be used with caution. Children must get first hand experience before using photocopiables. The photocopiable can be used to record understanding later. It works best as a small group activity with informed adult support.

Chapter 4

Using Artefacts in the Classroom

Learning outcomes

- To know what is and is not an historical artefact.
- To understand the difference between genuine artefacts (primary sources) and replica/reproduction artefacts (secondary).
- To be able to identify the skills used in investigating artefacts.
- To know how to develop these skills with children.

You will need:

- An historical artefact such as a domestic item from the first 50 years of the 20th century (Task 1).
- Access to the Internet or a book on Ancient Egypt (Optional Task).

What are artefacts?

An artefact is a manufactured object and therefore items such as fossils would not fall into this category. Artefacts can be used in the classroom in a range of contexts other than for history, for example religious education, art and geography. Whatever the subject focus, the process of the investigation will be the same. Primary teachers are advantaged because they have subject specialism in more than one area and can therefore focus more clearly on the specific subject area they are working in, while remaining mindful of work carried out with artefacts in other subject areas. For example, the investigation of an historical artefact which has religious meanings for some people requires the teacher and children to draw on their work in other subject areas such as RE and geography.

Objects as artefacts include paintings, sculpture, pottery, tools, coins, carvings and remains of buildings.

Artefacts for primary pupils

Artefacts provide key source material for developing children's awareness about life in the past. They may be:

- real original objects

- replicas

- real original objects seen in museums behind glass

- photographs of real original objects.

It is unlikely that children studying the Romans, Anglo-Saxons, Vikings, Tudors, ancient Greece or a world study of a past society are likely to have any real original artefacts in front of them. Even replicas tend to be so expensive that they are looked at from afar, just as they might be looked at in a museum. Photographs are by far the most common way in which KS2 children investigate artefacts, except when they study Britain since 1930 and the local study unit. This makes it very important for them to have had experience investigating real objects and building up a series of skills and questions which enable them to turn a photograph into an artefact in their mind's eye. Children need to know the size of photographic objects for example and may need help in identifying the materials from which the artefact is made.

Photographs

The skilful teacher has to enthuse children about the photographs of artefacts they see in books, on the Internet and on posters. Children have to be able to imagine the real artefact in front of them and ask the questions which will provide them with additional evidence about the past. Most photographs of artefacts are named, so the questions asked of it must move on from 'guessing its purpose' to looking for the information it gives us about the past. This allows children to work as historical detectives, but it only works well if the teacher and children have transferred a two-dimensional image into a three-dimensional one and it leaps off the page to sit or stand by the child.

There are some very successful design and technology schemes which build on this idea and engage children in construction and designing artefacts from the past, based on photographs.

Replicas

As children get older a distinction needs to be made between a real original object, such as a Victorian toy, and a replica. In this case the replica has the distinct advantage that it can be played with and explored as a toy. Older pupils will often point out constructional points that conflict with the idea that the toy could have come from the Victorian era.

Museums

Many good museums provide children with opportunities to touch and handle objects 'behind the scenes'. They also often provide good inservice courses for teachers, so that they can experience handling artefacts at first hand and use their skills in their own classrooms. Often, however, the museum visit involves looking at artefacts within a glass case. Good observational drawing is a key skill for this to be successful. Avoid the temptation to rush children past as many cases as possible, so they come back having learned very little about anything they have seen.

Photographs and postcards prior to the visit can help. Different groups of children can focus on different objects. The observational drawings can then be used back in the classroom as a starting point for investigating the artefact.

English Heritage have produced an excellent teacher's guide *Learning from Objects* (Durbin *et al.* 1990) which has sections on a rationale for using objects, learning from objects, using objects across the curriculum, developing skills for working with objects, thinking about things and a good bibliography. It is aimed at secondary, rather than primary, teachers but can be easily adapted and, most importantly, is easy to read.

Using artefacts in the classroom

Context

Children can be introduced to the idea that artefacts provide us with clues and evidence about the past. This can be done in one of two ways: either the object is named and its use described, or an unnamed object can be used. Work on an unnamed object can be a means of teaching children how to pose questions about artefacts. Both ways of using objects are valid and children need to have plenty of experience of both.

Making a checklist

A checklist can help children to find clues about an object. It also enables an adult other than the teacher to work effectively with a small group. The responses to the checklist can be oral or, as children become more proficient at writing, they can be recorded. Older children should be encouraged to draw up their own checklist based on physical features, constructional features, function and design. The one below is a guide for pupils at KS1 and the lower end of KS2.

Part A: Description

1. What does it look like?

2. What does it feel like?

3. What is it made from?

4. What does it smell like?

5. What colour is it?

Part B: Deduction

6. Does it look like anything we have seen before?

7. What is/was it?

8. How old is it?

9. Who used it?

10. Can we get a clue from another source, e.g. a book/another artefact that might go with it?

An observational drawing at this stage can help develop visual skills and provide a record of artefacts seen and touched.

The replies to the questions on a checklist involve developing a technical vocabulary to describe objects. Many of these words form essential historical concepts. Words such as 'old' and 'new' are relative. A replica 1950's carpet beater may be new, but it is representing something that is old. Historical word lists can help here:

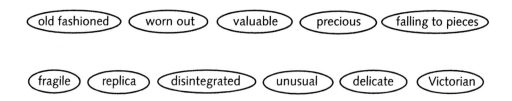

old fashioned   worn out   valuable   precious   falling to pieces

fragile   replica   disintegrated   unusual   delicate   Victorian

Use an historical artefact such as a domestic item from the first 50 years of the 20th century. Use pictures if you cannot access a real object. Go through the questions on the checklist. Then decide on a specific age range in your chosen key stage and decide:

- What prior learning would the children need to bring to a session which used this artefact?

- What vocabulary would you want them to have opportunities to use as a result of investigating the object?

- What other resources might you find useful, such as word cards, non-fiction texts? Give details of these.

- What would you expect most children to achieve through investigating the artefact?

- What would you expect from less able children?

- What would you expect from higher attaining children?

Compare your responses with those of someone else who has looked at a different key stage. Can you find evidence of progression in the teaching?

(Optional) Repeat the same activity using a photograph of an artefact from Ancient Greece or by accessing the Ancient Greek Exhibition on the British Museum website www.british-museum.ac.uk/

Sorting artefacts

A collection of artefacts can be used as a sorting activity, mimicking the archaeologist in the field. This sorting process can start at a very simple level, such as using the age of the object as a sorting category – a flat iron, 1950's iron, present day iron. The checklist above provides additional categories for sorting, so children can gain practice at looking for particular properties, for example the material the artefacts are made from. Sorting can be done according to texture, colour, use and age.

Sequencing artefacts

Artefacts can be used to develop children's awareness of changes in artefacts over time. Artefact timelines can be created. A very simple one would record artefact changes in the child's own life.

Toys I had when I was a baby
Toys I had when I was in nursery
My favourite toy today

Artefacts with stories

Not all adults and children enjoy the mystery object guessing games. Inanimate objects become more interesting when they are part of a story. The story may concern:

- The use of the object, e.g. someone showing how a cobbler's last was used and describing how they had their shoes repaired at home when they were young

- Devising a story about who has used the object, e.g. a Roman coin, purchased in a shop

- Devising a story about how a museum object came to be in the museum. (Bradman and Dupasquier's *The Sandal*, 1990 does this particularly well.) Many museums have easy access to records about the histories of their different collections. This makes a good homework task, for example asking KS2 children to explore how a particular collection – e.g. Greek vases/statues – came to be in the local museum. Older children can discuss the 'theft' of such treasures and whether they should be returned to their place of origin.

- Telling the story of how the object came into the classroom, e.g. 'I bought this on Sunday from a car boot sale/my grandfather lent me this to show you'.

The artefact becomes more personal and for many children more interesting. This is particularly true for artefacts that children themselves bring into school. One of the authors of this guide asked some children to bring in any objects they had which told us something about life in the 1960s. One child brought in a pickled gallstone, which his grandad had had removed. This certainly helped to personalise all those stereotyped textbooks about what life was like in the 1960s!

Collections of artefacts

Collections of artefacts linked to specific themes provide good visual and tactile evidence for children. Some themes can be very wide, such as the 1970s, or more specific, such as a display of objects used during the Second World War.

1. Bag games

There are a variety of mystery bag games which involve children in looking at collections of objects and suggesting what evidence they provide. These provide practical experience in interpreting evidence.

The feely bag game can have a historical perspective if children are asked to describe and recognise objects which may be linked with a historical theme.

Interpreting evidence from artificially constructed collections can be useful in raising cross-curricular issues such as gender stereotyping. A sports bag could belong to a man or a woman. Children are more likely to think it belongs to a man.

2. Houses

A quiz show on television took contestants round a famous person's house and asked them to use the evidence to guess whose home it was. Everyone's house provides evidence about who lives there. Shops, places of work, churches and temples all have artefacts that provide us with clues about the people who use the building. Young children need plenty of practice exploring present-day artefact clues before they can make informed decisions about evidence from the past. Older pupils need support from non-fiction texts to breathe life into artefacts. This is particularly true when artefacts from the period come as fragments in photographs.

3. Miscellaneous

- Spot the artefact in a visual source – book, photo, picture, advert.

- Stimulus for drama and role-play – re-creating the making, use or discovery of the artefact.

- Link an example to a historical story and use it as a story aid.

- Story stimulus – Who found it? Where? How did it come to be there? etc.

- Use in structured play context, e.g. Victorian Parlour – use artefacts such as sugar tongs; Victorian school room – use slates and chalk.

Collecting artefacts

1. School resources

- Collections built up around popular historical themes, e.g. toys, homes, holidays, famous people, washing, celebrations

- Forgotten resources – cupboards under stairs. Yesterday's scrap becomes today's historical artefact

2. Own resources
- Personal artefacts
- Purchased artefacts – car boot sales, flea markets, house clearance shops
- Attics and cellars
- Family and friends

3. Commercial
- School purchasing catalogues
- Shops such as **Past Times**
- Museum shops

4. Loan collections
- From museums, LEAs, libraries
- From Development Education Centres

5. Re-created
War toys made from scrap (for example)

1930's toilet paper from newspaper

6. Parents, local community
- Requests via the children
- Adverts in free newspapers
- School newsletters
- Local collectors willing to bring in and talk about their collection.

Artefacts as partial records of the past

Artefacts, like all sources of historical evidence, are only partial representations of the past. Although this is very obvious, it is often difficult for children to understand. One way in which some sort of introduction can be provided is to involve pupils in making choices about what they would choose to fill a suitcase, shoebox and so on which would represent lives of children today. Some schools and communities have done this practically by burying a time capsule, but teachers can simply raise it as a means of showing how limited our knowledge of the past is. Children can be asked to draw their collection of objects to inform future children about life at the start of the 21st century.

List six items you would include in a small suitcase to represent children's lives at the start of the 21st century. Now list another six items which could represent children's lives at the start of the 20th century. You may find it easier to concentrate on a particular aspect, e.g. school. What major gaps are there?

21st Century

1.

2.

3.

4.

5.

6.

20th Century

1.

2.

3.

4.

5.

6.

Archaeology and artefacts

Stories about the work of archaeologists can provide children of all ages with an insight into archaeology. The finding of Tutankhamen's tomb by Howard Carter is one of the most popular stories and can be used in both key stages. Both television and newspapers report archaeological discoveries and these can be used for exploring report reading and writing in the Literacy Hour as well as looking at the historical evidence they provide about the past. Other archaeologically linked activities could include:

- putting pieces of a broken pot together

- providing one fragment (e.g. a handle) and asking children to draw the rest of the pot

- a simulated dig (washing up bowl filled with soil and buried items; children use brush and small trowel).

(Optional) Visit Cairo museum on http://www.akhet.freeserve.co.uk/cairo.htm or look at photographs in a book of Carter's findings in Tutankhamen's tomb. What evidence do they provide about the daily life of the very wealthy at the time of Tutankhamen's death?

Chapter 5

Visual Sources: Photographs and Portraits

Learning outcomes

- To know the range of visual sources for pupils at both key stages.

- To be able to plan questions and activities which promote historical learning through visual sources at the relevant key stage, focusing on photographs and portraits.

- To understand some of the problems associated with visual sources.

You will need

A photograph of yourself taken some years ago (Tasks 1 and 2); black and white photograph of a Victorian school room (Task 3); a KS2 pupil text book about the Tudors with a picture of Henry VIII or Elizabeth I (Task 4); a photograph of the local area taken 100 years ago (optional task).

Range of visual sources

The term 'visual sources' covers a wide range of historical sources. These include photographs, paintings, portraits, advertisements, postcards, book illustrations, television, engravings, cartoons, sketches, pictures on pottery, pictures on stamps, pictures on song sheets, statues, coins and carvings. In this chapter we look at photographs and portraits, but most of the information and many of the teaching strategies can be used for work on the other visual sources. It is worth making a distinction between pictures, which are generally secondary sources of evidence, and photographs, which make us an eyewitness to an occasion. Illustrations in some picture books such as Janet and Allan Ahlberg's *Peepo* (1983) can provide good visual evidence.

Photographs

 Find a photograph of yourself taken some years ago. Affix it to the middle of a sheet of plain A4 paper (A3 if it is a very big photograph!). Now ask someone else to write down what evidence they can gather from this photograph about you. When they have written down five facts, ask them to illustrate what they think was 'outside the frame' (the parts not seen), when the photograph was taken. Of course, one of the things that was outside was the photographer! What difference does the photographer make to the photograph as a source of evidence?

Old photographs, particularly of the recent past, are not difficult to find. Packs of photographs on different topics, such as homes, the seaside, the 1960s, the Second World War and Victorian life, have been produced by a number of publishers. There is also a wealth of local photography available, sometimes in books about the local community, but often sold as postcards. Most schools have good collections of local photographs and of the school itself over a number of years. Photographs taken in and around the school over a period of time provide a useful resource for very young children. Teachers and pupils can then share the context within which they were taken, for example children in the playground in autumn, winter, spring and summer.

(Optional) Look at a photograph of your local area taken 100 years ago. Draw four columns, labelling them 'Now', 'Then', 'Change', and 'Continuing'. Record your observations in the relevant column. Then make comparisons between the area now and as it appeared in the photograph. What things have changed? What remains the same?

Now	Then	Change	Continuing

Using photographs in the classroom*

It is easy to make assumptions that when children look at photographs, or indeed any visual source, they see what we see, but some children enter school with a very limited experience of picture reading and their skills need developing. Work on 'reading pictures' is carried out as part of learning to read and children talk about illustrations and coloured photographs in early reading books. This is built and developed in subjects such as history, geography and religious education. These subjects look at pictures much more critically. Through them, children learn to interpret pictures, to look for visual bias and the hidden bias of visual sources.

Photographs, whether in colour or black and white, are essential for transmitting information and children will need help to 'read' them as 'non-fiction' in the same way they 'read' their early reading scheme books as 'fiction'. Black and white photographs may seem very dark and dismal to children who live in a colourful and fast moving world.

Several picture books exist that ask children to look carefully at pictures in order to discover hidden images. One of the most useful series is the fairly adult *Where's Wally?* by Martin Handford. This makes an excellent start to a structured programme of picture reading. The book can be cut up, put on card and laminated and then the children work in pairs to 'Find Wally'. Handford provides lists at the back of the book of other objects to be found in each picture. These can be cut out and stuck to the back of the card to provide extension activities for those children who have little difficulty finding Wally. This is an activity which works as well for Y6 as it does for reception children. Children can be asked what strategies they use to find Wally – random, systematic in small blocks, working from left to right in 'rows' or in 'columns'.

*This section is adapted from Hughes (1993) *Teaching History*.

The 'can you find' approach can be used as a starting point with other photographs. Return to the photograph you used for Task 1. What features could you ask someone to look for, which would provide them with evidence about you and/or the event which the photograph records?

Historical terms and vocabulary

Children may need help with historical terms to describe some of the features they can see in photographs, for example ration book, gas mask, dolly peg. Colour photographs of Greek buildings would require children to know words such as sculpture, column, frieze, capital. Photographs of Elizabethan houses would require specialist terms such as long-gallery and buttery. If you have chosen a photograph of your graduation ceremony, children would need help with words such as mortar board, graduation, graduate, scroll and gown.

Sequencing photographs

Sets of photographs can be taken which involve children in time sequencing as they determine which picture comes first. Five photographs taken during the school day/ week/year make a good starting point as children decide which photograph comes before which. Later, degrees of uncertainty may be introduced, for example a scene of children lining up may be morning or afternoon. The clues for the 'right' answer may not exist. Older pupils can sequence photographs of household objects, such as washing implements over the past 100 years (Victorian era and Britain since 1930), or photographs of monarchs (Tudors, Windsors).

Developing skills for 'reading' photographs*

The following strategies are recommended for children who have not had much experience of using photographs as historical evidence. They provide a framework within which to develop observational skills as well as more specific historical ones. They have been carried out with nursery, Key Stage 1 and 2 children.

1. Examine a recent colour photograph of a pupil or pupils and ask questions such as the following:

- Where was the photograph taken?

- When was it taken?

- Who is in it?

- What are they doing?

- Is the photograph posed, or are those in it unaware that they were being photographed?

- How do the children themselves pose in photographs?

- How does this relate to photographs being used as evidence?

It is important to note that we do not necessarily know the answers to all these questions.

2. Look at a commercial colour photograph of a reconstruction such as an Anglo-Saxon village, a Victorian kitchen or classroom. Similar questions to those above can be asked. Some children are very observant and will notice things that the teacher misses. Non-readers and less-able readers are often particularly good at spotting visual clues. When the teacher is sure that they are all 'seeing' the same thing, then some comparisons can be drawn between one of the colour photographs and children's own experiences – a local village, their own kitchen/classroom.

3. Black and white photographs can be used with groups in a similar fashion, making sure that children are actually seeing what is in each of the photographs. It may be helpful to provide a series of questions for each picture, drawing the children's attention to key elements in the photographs. These questions can be at different levels, put on to colour coded question cards. Children themselves can be invited to set questions as well as answer them.

---

*This section is adapted from Cox and Hughes (1990) *Starting History Photopacks*.

4 Find a black and white photograph of a Victorian school room. Plan a series of activities that would help a Y3 class to interpret the photograph.

What prior learning would be helpful?

What specific vocabulary would they need to describe the contents of the picture?

What questions would you ask if you wanted children to explore historical concepts such as chronology, change, continuity, similarity, difference, evidence and cause and effect?

Compare your questions with those of a colleague. Discuss what historical skills are being explored.

Portraits

Portraits are one of the most accessible forms of historical picture source material. English Heritage have produced an excellent guide to their use (Susan Morris, 1989). She describes portraits as the gossip columns, newsflashes, party political broadcasts and family albums of long ago before photography, television and other technologies could record or transmit images. Morris sees decoding the messages of portraits as vital in drawing evidence from the past.

The ideal way of working with portraits is to visit an art gallery where an Education Officer has developed a programme of historical portrait work for primary children of different ages. For reception children, this may involve looking at how children are represented in family portraits. They can make comparisons between their own clothes, toys and pets and those of the children in the portrait. Older pupils can look at Tudor portraits, Victorian narrative painting (of famous historical scenes) or representations of Greek myths and legends. Local galleries may also be useful for landscapes of the area, prior to photography.

Visits to art galleries may be ideal but are often not possible, particularly when schools are some distance from galleries that contain portraits for the relevant period. Teachers can provide alternative methods of helping children to 'read' portraits. A collection of postcards showing portraits can be used and some art galleries produce posters of pictures in their collection which are relevant to the Programme of Study for KS2. The Walker Art Gallery (telephone 0151 478 4199) in Liverpool for example has full sized posters of Elizabeth I and Henry VIII, which are used in many schools in the region. The National Portrait Gallery (020 7306 0055) has an extensive collection of cards and posters, including sets of postcards and teachers' notes to cover the study units for KS2. It is useful to do this as a directed teaching activity before the children move on to more individual interpretations from books or websites.

Starting points for using portraits

Either work with the whole class with a poster or have groups of children, working in pairs, using a series of postcards. It is easier if some of the postcards are the same, so that one pair of children can compare their findings with another pair.

The following questions are suggested by Morris (1989) and can be adapted for different age groups. Morris defines a portrait as meaning a work for which there was a consciously posed sitting by a person or group, and in which the sitter's identity is the main object of study.

 Find a photograph of a portrait of Henry VIII or Elizabeth I in a book about the Tudors and answer these questions. It is also possible to access these images through the National Portrait Gallery's search engine on http:www.npg.org.uk/search.

- Describe the sitter's clothes. What is the person wearing? Why?

- Describe the sitter's facial expression/mood.

- Describe the sitter's pose or gesture. What do these imply?

- Do you think the artist has shown the body's proportions well?

- Describe the background and accessories. What might these signify?

- What medium has the artist used, and what effect does this have?

- Has the artist used colours/textures or lighting effects in a special way?

- How large is the work? Does it have any effect on you?

- Does the frame show any special details?

- What is the sitter's name?

- What is the artist's name and the date?

Symbols and what they tell us

Animals, flowers and objects have symbolic meanings. There are dictionaries of these and also the traditional attributes of saints and gods. These help us to 'read' portraits and would have been familiar to those viewing the portraits at the time they were painted. Common symbols found in Tudor portraits include the Tudor rose, pillars and/or drapes, Turkish carpets and rich jewellery to add grandeur and strength to the sitter's image. Ships and stormy weather indicate Britain's prowess on the seas and the general expansion of Empire. Elizabeth I is wearing a brooch in the form of a pelican in the portrait of her in the Walker Art Gallery. The pelican was supposed to peck at its own breast to feed its young if there was no food. The message of the Pelican Portrait is that Elizabeth so loved her people that she would die in order to feed them. The Tudor monarchy was particularly effective at using portraits as a public relations exercise and any sequence of portraits showing either Henry or Elizabeth demonstrates this very clearly. A class of Y1 pupils who looked at a portrait of Elizabeth, without knowing who she was, were able to tell one of the authors of this guide that this woman was old, rich, important, frightening and cruel.

Interpreting and evaluating the evidence

The next stage from this descriptive process is to enable children to develop strategies for looking at visual material as historical evidence. This involves moving from description to questioning the images that are provided. Whether using photographs or portraits it is important to question why the image was made. Your graduation photograph has a very distinct purpose – to record you on the day. The clothes you are wearing are not typical of the clothes you normally wear, even though your photograph may show a number of other people wearing the same clothes. You may be holding a scroll, but this may be an empty piece of paper, which moves from one sitter to another.

In the past, only the very wealthy had their portraits painted and this was not only a record for posterity, but also public relations and myth making. The less wealthy of the distant past may be represented on engravings and line drawings which have survived, but the messages are more confused. Sometimes portraits of the poor or enslaved have been done to provide 'evidence' of their good treatment; for example there is a portrait of some very healthy looking pensioners in a Liverpool workhouse in the Walker Art Gallery. This makes a statement about the workhouse trustees, rather than the conditions of the workhouse.

Some other points to look for are:
- **Race and gender stereotyping** – the ways in which non-European peoples and communities and women are presented. White women do appear in many of the early photographs, just as they appear in portraits and sculptures but they tend to be in particular poses.

- **Invisibility and marginalising** – the absence of particular groups: the poor, non-European communities, women and children. The question of access is an important one. Early portrait painters and photographers were almost always white, wealthy men and the images they have created are the images of the world as they saw it.

- **Censoring reality/re-creating history** – particularly true with photography, when individuals have been edited out of photographs. Stalin, for example, had Trotsky taken out from many official photographs. Many portraits also show evidence of such editing. In some cases individuals or symbols have been painted over, dresses heightened to maintain the original sitter's modesty or the sitter has not favoured an ageing version of themselves. Elizabeth I's face remains much the same over several decades of portraits. There is nothing new in this. Visitors to the tomb paintings at Thebes can see examples of how Ancient Egyptian priest-politicians, thousands of years ago, ordered the destruction of images of Pharaohs whose views were no longer 'acceptable'.

- **Limited viewpoints** – portraits and photographs tend to show the expected: the photograph of the 1950's kitchen with everything looking clean and tidy; the picture of a reconstructed Victorian parlour in a museum, which shows everything the museum has to display.

- **Avoiding controversial issues** – particularly local issues in primary schools, where new housing estates and shopping malls may be sprawling over rich agricultural land, while the local run-down industrial estate looks much the same as it did twenty years ago.

- **Language** – captions on photographs and photographs of portraits.

- **Commercial interests** – photographers and artists being more concerned to produce a pleasing picture which would sell, rather than reflect reality.

- **Absence of direct observation** – portraits may not have been drawn or painted on the spot. Illustrations and later paintings from the illustrations may have been done from eyewitness accounts or even left to the artist's imagination. There are at least eight different portraits of Christopher Columbus, for example, because he was never painted in his lifetime.

- **Images intended to present a particular viewpoint** – such as those in the 19th century used by Dr Barnado, who ran a massive photographic campaign to raise money for his children's homes. He was eventually taken to court for his 'advertising' methods. A charity worker at the time said that Dr Barnado was not satisfied with taking photographs of children as they really were when they entered the homes, so he would tear their clothes 'to make them appear worse than they really are. They are also taken in purely fictional positions'.

The key message is that good history teaching helps children to interpret the visual images presented to them which represent the past. Teachers raise questions which children can then use, not only in history, but in their own daily lives.

Chapter 6

Written Sources

Learning outcomes

- To identify a number of different types of historical written sources.

- To attain the ability to use a variety of written sources to promote children's historical knowledge and skills.

You will need

A selection of personal written records, including your birth certificate (Task 3)

Range of written sources

Written sources take a variety of different forms, both printed and handwritten – government records, local records, personal records, newspapers and musical scores. In this chapter we look at the first three forms in more detail. Written sources are a key form of primary historical source material for the British study units Victorian Britain and Britain since 1930. Many schools combine their local study with one of these units, which means that the local study can access original written source material and the relevant study unit can be examined in greater depth. One of the most useful sources of information about using documents is the English Heritage Guide by Ian Davies and Chris Webb (1996). It covers documents relating to housing, health, poverty, population, work, leisure, religion and education.

Written sources at KS1

Written sources are also important at Key Stage 1 – and for the under fives. The emphasis may be on English, rather than history, but unless children understand the historical/ religious/geographical context they will remain functionally illiterate, i.e. they can read the words, but have no understanding about the content.

History, literacy and written sources

History provides a wealth of genuine non-fiction texts for children to explore – lists, signs, labels, captions, personal recounts of visits and events, diaries, journals, political pamphlets, letters, certificates, invitations, adverts, newspapers. For younger and less-able readers, most documents will need transcribing, but any historical document requires children to synthesise and evaluate its contents as well as recount the contents. The genuine written source – the report, the certificate, the logbook – becomes an artefact as well as a written source. Four-year-olds who hold their school's Victorian logbook or look at it when they go into the headteacher's room will remember its weight, its smell and the strange writing. At seven, they may be able to recognise some of the words. By 11, they should be able to read and understand the content and context of most pages.

Government records

Census returns

KS1 – Periodically householders fill in an electoral register form which asks who lives in the household and who will be 18 or older on a specific date. As the form asks for very little information it is probably one of the most accessible written sources for younger primary children. It shows how information about individuals living in a house is documented and used by officials.

Census forms are much more complex and often very difficult to read. Local historical societies and libraries have often interpreted some of the material on census forms, so that it is not necessary to spend hours wading through micro-film in the local library. Older pupils may enjoy doing this, particularly if their family has lived in the area for some time. Several websites have been developed to enable individuals to trace their ancestors e.g. http://www.genealogy.bookpub.net (Trace your family roots).

This is an extract from a genuine census form in Liverpool at the end of the 19th century. Do the task with at least one other person, so that you can discuss the information you collect and deduce.

- What information does it give the reader?

- What does it tell you about the movements of people?

- Who lives at 25 Moses Street?

- How many children are in the family?

No. of Schedule	Street	Name	Relation to head of family	Condition	Age last birthday – males	Age last birthday – females	Occupation	Where born
284	25 Moses St	Henry Cowan	Head	Mar	36		Seaman	Bermuda
		Louisa Cowan	Wife	Mar		29		Bristol
		Katherine	Dau			10		Bristol
		Henry Cowan	Son		8			Bristol
		George Cowan	Son		5			Bristol
		Marie Cowan	Dau			3		Liverpool
		Edith Cowan	Dau			1		Liverpool
		Child unchristened	Dau			1 month		Liverpool
		Caroline Jackson	Mother In-Law	Mar				Falmouth
		George	Brother	Unmar	33		Seaman	Bermuda

If you were using this extract with children you could ask them to draw a picture of the family, with the help of non-fiction texts, and write the first names under each person. Older children could draw a family tree. They could all speculate on why a month old baby did not have a name. Computers have made collections of data much more manageable, but interpretation of data remains a key thinking skill.

Local records

These include school, church, local government, inventories, political pamphlets, street and trade directories, maps and plans and local newspapers.

School-related

Many of these are school-based and are easy to access, for example the school logbook, punishment book, minute books, school accounts, school rule books, school registers, timetables, magazines and newspaper cuttings.

The logbook is probably the most fascinating. It is kept by the headteacher to record important events that take place at the school. The most fascinating logbooks are held in schools that have been in existence for many years. They hold information about inspectors' reports, names of staff and managers, late arrivals, truancy, lesson outlines and standards, comments about the weather and significant events in the life of the school. It is often the similarity, rather than the difference, which strikes the adult reader. The 1880's inspection sounds remarkably similar to the 2000 one!

 Ideally, this activity should be undertaken, or discussed, with someone from a different key stage. It then becomes possible to compare activities and see how the same written source can be revisited at a later stage and mark a progression in children's learning.

Extract from a school logbook

2.6.53   *The Assembly Hall and three classrooms were fitted with television sets. All pupils unable to see the Coronation at home were invited into school. Thus every child on the School Roll, saw Her Majesty, Queen Elizabeth crowned.*

3.6.53   *Coronation Party held at the school with entertainers provided by the U.D.C and games and competitions organised by Teaching staff.*

5.6.53   *The Chairman of the Managers presented each pupil with a Coronation Souvenir Pencil.*

9.6.53   *The School Coronation Festival presented to an audience of 530 parents in the open air. The programme included Maypole Dancing, Country Dancing, A Mass P.T. Display and a pageant of England through the ages.*

- Devise two activities for a Y2 class using part of this extract, or devise two activities for a Y6 class using the whole extract.

- Use the Attainment Target levels in the National Curriculum to identify an activity which would access the children's understanding of the logbook as an historical source.

What prior knowledge would pupils need prior to carrying out the activities? What additional historical sources could be used to enrich children's interest and understanding?

The daily register provides an ever-present example of a continuing record of school attendance and children can see for themselves the records of their absences. In some schools attendance certificates are given to children with a 100 per cent attendance rate and these can be compared with certificates issued to children in the past. Looking at certificates children already hold is a good way of interesting them in written sources as a form of historical evidence. What would these certificates tell us if they were found in a desk in 20 years' time?

Victorian and Edwardian timetables can provide an opportunity to compare activities undertaken now with those in the past. Some subjects such as 'object' lessons have disappeared, but may be more familiar to children than they think.

Parish and church registers

These show that many adults in the nineteenth century were unable to write their own names and marked their signatures with an X. The high rate of infant mortality is also evident from parish records and graveyards. Children doing a local study using their local churchyard often have very perceptive responses for the reasons for this. In some areas infant mortality is still an issue and a surprising number of children have families where an infant death or miscarriage has taken place.

Church records are often used by people who want to trace their own family tree.

(Optional – Key Stage 2) What information does this table give about members of the Doddsworth family who died between 1790 and 1812?
Devise some questions for pupils doing a local study of Waterside.

Date of Death	Surname	Christian Name	Name of Parent or Widower	Trade or Profession	Place	Age	Cause of Death
26.7.1811	Doddsworth	Hannah	Jno		Waterside	3 days	Decline
1.3.1810	Doddsworth	Margaret	James	Weaver	Waterside	3 days	Decline
19.8.1812	Doddsworth	Martha	John	Weaver	Waterside	2	Smallpox
1.11.1807	Doddsworth	Mary	John	Weaver	Waterside	1	Whooping Cough
1.5.1811	Doddsworth	Michael	Willm	Weaver	Waterside	6 mths	Fever
25.1.1800	Doddsworth	Nancy	Willm	Weaver	Waterside	2	Worms
9.11.1792	Doddsworth	Ralph		Soldier	Waterside	96	Old Age
26.8.1802	Doddsworth	Sally	John	Weaver	Waterside	8 wks	Fits
14.8.1785	Doddsworth	Sarah		Widow	Waterside	59	Cancer
2.6.1803	Doddsworth	Sarah	Jas	Weaver	Waterside	14 wks	Fits
3.3.1798	Doddsworth	Susan	John	Weaver	Waterside	20 wks	Decline
10.6.1790	Doddsworth	Susanna			Waterside	Inft.	Smallpox

Trade directories

A variety of trade directories exist which set out the names and occupations of traders in a particular area. The further back in time these directories go the more likely it is that they will contain occupations and trades which no longer exist. Children may, however, recognise the trades from books they read or have had read to them. Extracts from local directories are particularly useful for KS2 children studying the Victorian era, Britain since 1930 and/or a locality study. They can investigate them, alongside photographs of streets, and record changes in shop use over a period of time.

Today's *Yellow Pages* have replaced these directories and can be used to make more generic comparisons between local trades – 50 years ago/100 years ago. This can be done for either of the British Study Units on the Victorians or Britain since 1930 or a local study.

Street and place names, inn signs and local maps

Street and place names can provide another source of information about the history of the area which the school serves – Castle Street, Mill Street, Railway Road, Bridge Street, Gas Works Lane. In the older parts of many cities, street names were often taken from the area from which many of the first inhabitants had come. Local and national dignitaries often had streets named after them – Raglan Street in Burnley for example is surrounded by a number of other dignitary–named streets from the same era. Schools are often named after the street in which they are built and although this may seem obvious to us as adults some children do need to have it pointed out. Newer estates need more care: street names may reflect the whim of the builder rather than record local historical sites.

Old inn/pub signs often record a special history – famous events, river and canal names, sports, old pilgrim hostels, myths and legends, living creatures, railway inns, occupations, local connections and famous people. Even quite young children can make perceptive insights into pubs named 'The Victoria' and 'The Railway Arms'.

Local newspapers

Local libraries and local history associations usually have a good collection of locally collected resources, such as local newspapers and guide books going back several decades. Many local newspapers run a local history series, with photographs and extracts from the papers over a series of years. Researching these areas can be a good homework task for older and more-able KS2 pupils, who can then find out how these written sources are being transferred to modern technology and ways in which databases can be used for a local history study.

The millennium inspired a number of newspaper packages both local and national, which are useful (and cheap) for using with pupils. *The Times*, for example, has facsimiles for 1800 and 1900 and the 20th century in photographs.

Many record offices have published archive packs about topics and themes in their own area. They are usually aimed at interested adults, so teachers need to interpret and use them selectively for their own purposes. Some record offices provide supplementary material written especially for teachers and pupils.

Personal records

These include letters, diaries, wills, inventories, school reports, house plans and accounts.

 What information would your birth certificate give to someone who did not know you? Compare your birth certificate with someone else's. Does everyone in your family have the same form of birth certificate? What other historical evidence could be drawn from your personal written sources? Have you included letters, postcards, train tickets, newspaper cuttings and so on?

If you don't mind sharing personal sources with pupils this can be one of the most rewarding 'ways in' to using written sources. As with the evidence bags, it does help if you know more than the written sources reveal. It demonstrates how partial evidence is and also challenges divergent thinkers to create a story around the written source. Laminated colour photocopies make a good interactive display, particularly if interspersed with some photographs. Formal qualification certificates such as degree and post-degree awards provide a starting point for conversations about higher education – particularly important in areas where few parents have higher qualifications themselves. Car boot sales and house clearances are often a good source of personal records if you are not able to use your own.

School reports and personal items

One of the authors of this guide has a collection of school reports for a Lancashire family dated between 1920 and 1924, purchased for 50p from the Bygone Times warehouse in Eccleston, Lancashire. One of the things these reports do is to demonstrate how uninformative reports were in the 1920s!

Younger primary children often bring into school personal records in the form of birthday cards, postcards, letters from carers about visits to the dentist or time off through sickness or holiday. On an individual level these personal records are every bit as important historically as more traditional personal records. The baby books available on the market indicate that many people do keep on-going personal records of their children's progress and these are a wonderful source of material if carers are willing to share them with the class. It is often possible to photocopy extracts and so build up individual histories for children in the class. These may be linked to a timeline, or simply made into a book which can be kept in the class library, enabling present and future classes to see historical written sources.

The daily or weekly news records that many children are asked to make as part of their language programme can also be used as a historical source. The changes in writing and activities over a term provide a useful record of individual progress at Key Stage 1. At Key Stage 2, children can look at their own Records of Achievement and comment on the progress recorded there through its written sources.

Diaries

Diaries fall into two main groups. The first group contains diaries that have survived because their writers were famous. Extracts from these diaries can be used to supplement a story-telling session. They can include the diaries of the young, as well as the more famous diaries of people like Anne Frank and Samuel Pepys. Diaries of far more ordinary people have been published when they throw an unusual insight on the past. ✂

Postcards

Postcards have the advantage of being both a visual and written form of reference. Sometimes the picture supplements the written material and at other times bears no relation to the written source.

Inventories

Inventories provide a written record of the individual possessions of someone from the past. From the early 16th century, in order to provide a will the executors had to produce for the court a probate inventory. This was a list and valuation of all the moveable goods owned by the testator at the time of death. These can be extensive lists, particularly when recording the contents of large family houses, but often quite small localised ones can be found that illustrate very simply how few possessions people had in the past.

 (Optional – Key Stage 2) A true and lawful inventory of all the goods and implements of the household of Robert Leigh of Prescot, lately deceased, valued by three neighbours – Henry Brown, George Rochdale and John Chaddock – 24th April 1582

1 cow
1 horse
Brass and pewter
Frying pan and other iron
3 Pairs of sheets
2 Coverlets
3 Carts, 1 pair of wheels
7 Collars, 2 Packsaddles
Pots
Corn and grass on the ground
Treen ware and
1 coffer
Butter
Muck
Fuel
Backclothes

In which year was the inventory made? Whose inventory was it? Where did he live? Who valued his goods? What job do you think he had?

After you have answered these questions think of some questions that would require children to recall, select and organise historical information using non-fiction texts – Who was the monarch? Use a non-fiction text to help you draw Robert's house. What is treen ware? (wooden plates)

House plans and accounts

Key Stage 1 children may be drawing plans of their own classrooms and these can provide a useful record if furniture and displays are moved at a later date. The original plans then provide the historical evidence of how the classroom used to look. Many schools have original plans of their site and an investigation into the school as a historic site can involve looking at these and making comparisons between then and now and deductions about the reasons for different planning structures.

Comparisons of money between the present and the past are difficult. Written accounts prior to decimalisation complicate this further because they are shown in £ s d. However, young children can be introduced to the idea that written accounts provide some form of evidence from the past and older pupils can have some practice working in bases of 12 and 20. Often it is a good reminder that anyone now aged over 35 had to do this on a daily basis in school before currency was decimalised.

Chapter 7

TV, Film, Radio, ICT and Drama

Learning outcomes

- To identify the different forms of film that can promote historical skills, knowledge and understanding.
- To evaluate a schools' broadcast for the relevant key stage.
- To devise strategies for using TV and video as a stimulus for drama and role-play.
- To be aware of the different ways in which ICT can be used in history.

You will need

A copy of the *Times Educational Supplement (TES)*, the TV and radio section of a newspaper (Task 1); a video of a schools' history broadcast for the relevant key stage, National Curriculum Programme of Study for history (Task 2); QCA Guidelines on Speaking and Listening (Task 3); Landmarks video (Optional task). Access to a television and video.

TV, film and radio

There are six main types of TV, radio and film available for use in schools.

- Schools Broadcasts TV and radio for specific topics within the NC requirements which are accompanied by teachers' notes and can be recorded and kept. Many of these are now available for separate purchase, such as the BBC's Landmarks series. Schools often have a good collection of such broadcasts, although it may be harder to track down the relevant teachers' notes and pupil supports.

- Documentary programmes on children's TV, general TV or radio. These often include primary source material, oral history, photographs, written sources and film archive material. There are also documentary videos such as the North West Film Archive material.

- Designated history and 'discovery' channels.

- Commercially produced video material. Many local history associations are producing commercial videos on local history, steam engines, local ships and so on, which are stocked by WHSmith and other booksellers. Other companies, such as Pathe News, are producing commercial videos for specific years. These generally start in the 1930s.

- Film or TV fiction drama, such as Robin Hood, *The Secret Garden, The Railway Children, Oliver Twist,* Cartoon Shakespeare, *Tom's Midnight Garden.*

- CD-ROM and world wide web materials which include film archive.

1 **Look in the TV and radio section of the *TES*. Note down anything which you feel would be useful for history teaching at your key stage. Now turn to this afternoon's and evening's television programmes in your newspaper. Is there anything there which could be usefully adapted for history teaching at your key stage, or which would enhance your own subject knowledge?**

It is essential that you watch or listen to the material before showing it to the class. In recent research Croll *et al.* (Conference Paper presented in 1996) showed that two-thirds of primary teachers failed to do that, seriously affecting their ability to use the programme as a tool for teaching. Never let the programme do the history for you. The programme should be part of your teaching not the teaching itself. Use the teachers' notes which are a valuable source of information and ideas, but adapt the pupil sheets to meet the specific needs of your pupils. Do not be afraid to abandon the teachers' notes, if you find them unhelpful. As a student teacher you will need to have a lesson plan for a television programme. You need to be clear about the learning outcomes you wish to achieve through use of the programme, and be sure that the medium is the most effective way of delivering these outcomes.

How does the medium help?

1. It is a medium which is very familiar to children and they perceive it as a source of enjoyment rather than work. They should be well motivated. In order to avoid a 'zombie' approach to watching you will need to direct them towards watching with care and listening with attention. At first, you may find it useful to use the same sort of direct teaching as was suggested with photographs.

   - Prepare children for a short viewing session – five or ten minutes.

   - Provide a context and purpose for viewing.

- You may want to give the children some questions for which you will be seeking the answers after viewing.

- Re-play the extract and ask the children if they can think of additional questions. Turning children into active watchers can take some time, but is an essential life-skill.

2. For children with reading difficulties or with a class of early readers this material provides visual and oral access to historical sources of evidence, knowledge and ideas.

3. If on video, you have control of pace, length and timing, you can stop and ask questions, direct attention and lead discussions.

4. It provides children with a visual reconstruction of the past. This helps them to imagine a real past and gives support for their own historical role-play and drama.

To make effective use of the medium you need to identify a series of strategies that can be employed before, during and after using the medium. The chart below outlines a number of possible strategies.

Before	During	After
1. Promote enthusiasm for the medium	1. Identify and extract important information	1. Identify and extract information
2. Clarify purpose for its use, e.g. you may want to give children some questions for which you will be seeking the answers after viewing	2. Help children to identify how they can do this	2. Summarise structure of the programme
3. Identify need to concentrate on what is happening	3. Help them to organise the structure of the programme and the information provided	3. Draw conclusions
4. Link programme with something the children already know	4. Monitor the way in which the children are understanding and correct misconceptions	4. Make judgements and generalisations
5. Clarify any ideas or language which may be useful		
6. Identify other resources in the classroom linked to the programme		

Find a schools' history broadcast for a year group in your relevant key stage. Watch it, ideally with a few colleagues, and then answer the following questions.

- Is this programme suitable for the age and ability of children in the class?

- How does this programme fit in with the history Programme of Study?

- What knowledge, skills and understanding does it cover?

- What preparation would be needed in terms of preparing the children to watch the programme – knowledge, skills, questions?

- What would you want to focus on within the programme? It might help you to record two learning objectives for a lesson based on the programme and some questions which might help children's learning.

- What follow–up discussion or activities would come from it?

- If you were working with a mixed aged group – Yrs 1/2 or 5/6 – how would you differentiate the activities?

Now record:

1. The vocabulary the children would need to know prior to watching and the vocabulary they would learn as a result of watching the programme.

2. The additional resources you would need to support children's learning and motivation.

3. A role-play or drama activity follow-up which has a historical focus.

Film archive material

Series such as *Cine Memo, Out of the Dolls House, Time Watch* and *Pathe News* contain film archive material which can be used in part as a source of evidence. Many good reference CD-ROMS, including encyclopaedia, also contain film archive.

Use the material as you would any other source of evidence. What is happening? What does this tell us about life/an event in the past? Look for details of costume, transport, toys, houses and interiors.

As with photographs, remember that much of the surviving material, particularly news footage, was used for propaganda purposes or for instruction.

Fiction

The major problem with fiction film is authenticity. How accurate are the images portrayed? It is important for children to be told that this film is not from the past but has been filmed recently to tell a story set a long time ago. It is acted and is make believe. In general, modern film material, particularly children's TV fiction, is very accurate. Generally, the material in films made between the Forties and Sixties is not.

You can use extracts of adult films, and indeed comedy series set in the past, for example a castle interior or World War II home, but avoid showing too much. The children will get drawn into the story and want to see more!

 (Optional) Look through one of the Landmarks packs for KS2 History – Ancient Egypt, Tudor Times. Look at the units within the QCA Scheme of Work and identify ways in which the video could enhance the teaching of the unit. Can you think of any specific problems in using the video – with the whole class, with a group of children within the class?

History and ICT

There have been several central government publications on history and information technology. They date quickly and you are well advised to experiment with ICT yourself. Below are five ways in which ICT can be used in the classroom – whatever the age of the children.

1. History and the Web

The Web is a great educational resource, but it can be addictive and time-consuming. So take care and adopt a critical approach to the materials available. Sites change daily, new sites are added and some become out of date.

If you are a newcomer in looking for history sites, http://learnfree.co.uk provides a good starting point. From its initial site, click 'Teachers'. When you reach the Teachers site, click 'Reviews'. This will give you three choices. One of these is 'Best of the Web' and this will give you access to a number of different sites which are useful for teachers. If you click history it will give you access to museums, virtual tours, documents, etc. Three hours later you could have visited Pompeii, Cairo and the Egyptian and Greek sections of the British Museum, the Mary Rose and much much more. Museums, such as the British Museum, provide some useful sites for children. Some of these have been developed by schools, who have received funding to employ a professional to make sure the site is attractive and age specific. 'Best of the Web' will also give you access to central government agencies such as OFSTED and the DfEE.

General information sites about English Heritage, museum websites, etc. can be accessed on www.24hour museum.org.uk

Sites such as www.britannia.com/history focus on the UK and there are a number of other sites which look at specific Programmes of Study, e.g. www.roman-empire-net (with www.asterix.tm.fr for a lighter touch!) and www.control.chalmers.se/vikings; www.royal.gov.uk is the official royal website and starts in AD400. www.bbc.co.uk/radio4/sceptred isle analyses the era between 55BC and 1959.

A more general search is possible through the search engines supplied by the Internet provider. Typing in 'Castles' for example, will give you a list of castle websites and you can then click on any which seem useful for the topic you are studying. www.askjeeves.com can provide a good starting point. At the time of writing, this site had just been revamped to provide an enhanced UK context to its responses.

There are several sites on the web which offer lesson plans and activities. Some of these are very poor and consist of poor quality photocopiable sheets with black and white sketches of historical figures and events for pupils to colour.

2. History CD-ROMs

These are being up-dated all the time and most of us are dependent on what has already been bought by the school in which we are working. Again, 'Best of the Web' supplies reviews of software and this gives some limited guidance to what is available.

3. Encyclopaedia on CD-ROM

The quality varies considerably. There are useful study skills involved in locating the information from encyclopaedia on CD-ROM, but the resulting information needs to be processed. The reading levels are often very high and consequently of more use to adults than children. History non-fiction is one of the hardest genres to understand. Children can read the words, but the register and concepts may make it very difficult for them to understand.

4. Word-processing and DTP

Access to good word-processing facilities means that children's writing can be much more varied. Templates for different writing genres can be drawn up for younger pupils and older pupils can devise their own and experiment with different formats and genres. Non-fiction history texts can be used as models for children's own work. For example, moving from the very simple 'Now and Then' history picture books to the more complex double page spreads used in many KS2 history texts.

5. Databases and handling information

Databases may involve pupils:

- as users – interpreting databases such as census data, which have already been created;

- as creators – creating simple databases linked to data collected on a history topic, e.g. street survey, linked to census data for the same street.

QCA's *History Teachers' Guide Update* 2000 is more limited in its approach to using ICT in history. It identifies four areas in the use of ICT resources when planning for historical enquiries:
(i) Use CD-ROMs in Units 4, 6C, 13, 15; (ii) Use websites in Unit 20; (iii) Use e-mail in Units 9, 13; (iv) Sort, edit, reorganise and present information in Units 4, 12, 15.

Drama

The National Trust has used drama very successfully with primary schools to provide pupils of all ages with an opportunity to recreate the past for themselves. This increases their knowledge of the past and provides a forum for discussion about different ways of interpreting the past. The drama format enables pupils to demonstrate their ability to organise and communicate their understanding and knowledge and gives them access to a range of information which would not normally be available to them. It often raises important historical questions about daily life in the past, such as toilets, bathing, dress and working children.

Schools' broadcasts often model drama for children. Teachers can use and adapt these models to provide a drama/role-play format for those children who are not able to get the first-hand experience of working on a historic site with skilled players. Initially, teachers can look at the historical information provided by the broadcast and ask children to identify how the information has been obtained and if it is correct. The difference between fact and fiction is an important one at Key Stage 1. Teachers can discuss and record with the class what is true about the video drama or role-play, what is not true and what is uncertain. Interpretation of television broadcasts involving drama at KS2 gives opportunities for enquiry and investigation of sources. A play about a Victorian household, for example, involves looking at a number of different sources. Children's response to historical drama needs to include its veracity as well as its theatrical effects.

History is often the key context for teaching drama in the English Programme of Study. At KS1, this involves working in role, presenting drama and stories to others and responding to performances. At KS2 it covers improvisation and working in role, scripting and performing in plays and responding to performance (National Curriculum 1999). The QCA guidelines for teaching Speaking and Listening in KS1 and KS2 extend these. The guidelines suggest drama activities for each term of each year (Y1–6), recommend a focus for teaching and ways in which this focus can be extended and reinforced. Student teachers often start with the role-play of the Victorian school room, but with confidence can move on to cameos of Mary Seacole and the Crimean War (a Year 2 class observed during a recent OFSTED inspection) and Roman soldiers landing in Britain (a Year 3 class observed on teaching practice).

 Read through the Drama Activities section of the QCA document on teaching Speaking and Listening.

KS1 – Devise a role-play area which extends children's awareness of the past

or

KS2 – Devise an activity which enables pupils to explore 'through improvisation and role-play a different period of history' (Y5 T2).

Chapter 8

Music

Learning outcomes

- To identify the different kinds of music that can be used as historical source material.

- To develop skills in using teaching strategies which incorporate music as a historical source.

You will need

Music from the 1960s and a picture which shows how people danced to this music (Task 1). Illustrated Mother Goose Treasury (Task 2)

Music as an historical resource

Music is an integral part of our daily lives and so it is not surprising that music should be seen as a historical source. The National Curriculum for music for both key stages requires pupils to be taught musical knowledge, skills and understanding through 'a range of live and recorded music from different times and cultures'. It obviously makes sense that this section of the music curriculum is integrated with a historical context which is known to the children.

The presence of a music specialist in school is likely to influence how much music is used within the history Programme of Study, but even for the non-specialists there are several ways in which music can be used to enrich the Programme of Study.

- Songs, dances and music associated with a particular time in history.

- Songs, dances and recreated music from the more remote past.

- Children's rhymes and jingles from the past.

- Musical achievements of the past.

- Music for celebrations.

- Simple composition of sounds to mark the passage of time.

- Music as mood creation for simple historical drama.

Songs, dances and music associated with a particular time in history

It is relatively easy to get hold of music from the recent past which can be used for Key Stage 1 children and for children studying Britain since 1930. A decades project on the 1950s or 1960s for example can use the popular music of the period to show what people listened and danced to at the time. Access to this music is easy and the number of record and CD remakes mean that children are often familiar with it. Many record companies produce albums, cassettes and CDs with titles such as 'The best of the 1950s', 'Big Band Sounds of the 1940s'. These can be used to create mood music, but also provide important historical evidence for the many pictures and photographs showing leisure activities.

 Find one picture of couples dancing in Britain in the 1960s and some music that would enhance children's understanding of what was happening in the picture. What vocabulary would you need to introduce? Could you do the dance yourself and teach the children?

Songs, dances and recreated music from the more remote past

Access to these is becoming much easier as more publishers take up the challenge of recreating music from past times. Many, such as Oxford University Press, have made a deliberate attempt to support the Study Units at KS2. For the musically talented, there are publications which feature musical scores, so that children can not only listen but also have the opportunity to play music from the past. This in itself gives the opportunity to recognise that people in the past were creative and imaginative. A good recorder group, for example, who can play Greensleeves, can introduce a different element into a Study Unit such as Britain and the wider world in Tudor times. There are a number of paintings from the Tudor period which show musicians and dance. One of the most famous is that of the life story of Sir Henry Unton. The National Portrait Gallery has posters and cards of this delightful painting, which includes several domestic scenes as well as musicians and dancers. It can also be accessed on http:www.npg.org.uk/search

Children's rhymes and jingles from the past

Nursery rhymes have a long tradition and controversy has raged about the political message of many of their words. Others have a social meaning. For example, it comes as quite a shock to realise that the popular 'Ring a Ring of Roses' rhyme was linked with the plague. The ring of roses referred to the signs of the plague on the victim's body, the posies were the nosegays people carried to try and ward it off, sneezing was another symptom of the disease, and once the victims fell they never got up again. Alan Trussell-Cullen's *A Pocket Full of Posies* (1989) looks at the history of nursery rhymes and covers 24 different rhymes. Some like 'Old King Cole' can be linked to KS2 Study Units.

Many traditional rhymes have disappeared from the playground and have been replaced with jingles from television commercials and pop songs. There is, of course, a continuity between this and the old street cries used to persuade people to buy Hot Cross Buns and Muffins. Teachers are probably responsible for ensuring that each generation of children does have some knowledge of simple nursery rhymes and jingles which would otherwise vanish. Many picture books of nursery rhymes and jingles provide a rich visual source of historical illustrations. The words of the rhymes record traditions and times long gone.

 Look through a Mother Goose Treasury and find three rhymes and jingles which record life in the (more) distant past. What sort of vocabulary would children need to describe the pictures (KS1)? What record of a particular period of history do some of the rhymes demonstrate (KS2)?

Musical achievements of the past

Classical music

In the past classical music was dependent on the patronage of the rich, particularly the court, and many of the stories about composers record this tradition. The bi-centenary of Mozart's death, for example, produced several books on his life, including some picture books which are suitable for KS1 pupils. Catherine Brighton's (Brighton 2000) book on Mozart gives a good opportunity for teachers to read a story about someone famous from the past which can then be extended by playing some of his music. The exclusion of women from formal training makes it difficult to find female examples. The photographs and illustrations show instruments used in the past. Wealthy Victorian family portraits often show an array of musical instruments and a surprising number of far less wealthy households had a piano until well into the 20th century.

Folk songs

There is a strong tradition of folk songs among different communities and many give powerful recounts of events in the distant past. They often have local industrial links, with songs about weavers featuring in some areas, and coal-miners and pit disasters recorded in folk song. Song and music have been powerful methods of oral histories for centuries and in many cases are the only record of traditions and events in small, isolated communities.

Popular music

For many children, this provides an easier access to music as a historical source. Many of the traditional songs and accompanying music are reminders of a time when people were engaged in heavy, tedious and poorly paid work. Music was used as a means of encouraging them to get their tasks completed. The commercialisation of this music of labour should not hide the song's original history.

Much popular music today is truly multi-cultural as travel and communications have enabled musical traditions from all over the world to combine and merge together in new sounds. Sometimes the origins are easy to trace, but most of us are probably unaware of the debt we owe to struggling peoples over the world who produced music in order to survive and which may be the only record of their lives. Examples include negro spirituals, jazz, sea shanties, military music, street music and country dances.

The Victorians and music

Victorian philanthropists were responsible for providing buildings and sites for music all over the country. This gave access to music for a much larger number of people. They built Pavilions and Winter Gardens in their seaside resorts and inland spas and bandstands in parks and on promenades. This led to the growth in the number and size of concert orchestras, military and brass bands. These still exist today in some areas and some children may have members of their own families who play in a band.

Light opera, the music halls, choirs and choral singing were all popular in the 19th century and the growing middle classes took up music-making in their own homes in a way that had previously been restricted to the wealthy. By the 1920s, many working people had a piano in the front room and spent time and money encouraging their children to learn to play. Children who have grandparents and great grandparents in their 60s and 70s could ask them about this.

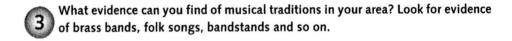 **What evidence can you find of musical traditions in your area? Look for evidence of brass bands, folk songs, bandstands and so on.**

Music for worship and celebrations

Music in many different forms is frequently associated with worship and celebrations. Behind traditional set pieces there are often good stories and the words themselves may record activities which have long since disappeared. Many carols sung at Christmas, for example, contain references to traditions which have vanished, such as wassailing. There exist songs and dances from all over the world for spring and harvest festivals, and music for carnivals. Frequently this music has strong historical roots.

Assemblies are often used as an opportunity for children to listen to music. When playing part of a recording it is better to 'fade down' music rather than stop it suddenly. Always tell the children what is being played and if there is a relevant historical context give information about this as well.

Simple composition of sounds to mark the passage of time

At the Foundation Stage and Key Stage 1, pupils can look at sound sources over a period of time. If they carry out a sounds environmental trail at different times of the year, this will give some sense of changes over a period of time. Recordings of bird song and animals can be used when it is unlikely that the local environment will produce these different sounds. This type of seasonal sound work can be extended to include songs about the seasons and playing short extracts from Vivaldi's 'The Four Seasons' and Delius's 'On Hearing the First Cuckoo in Spring'.

Music as mood creation for historical drama

1. Music as a historical source of evidence can be used to enhance a visit to a local building or site. A sea shanty sung in a maritime museum was used to create the atmosphere of working people on the docks for a local history project. Carols sung in a local church or cathedral reinforce the musical heritage of such sites.

2. One of the authors of this guide is a member of a historical dance group and when working in school held regular historical dance sessions for both Key Stage 1 and 2 pupils after school. Modern music, with a strong rhythmic movement, was used for the warm-up sessions, then the children were given a break to listen to some High Renaissance Dance Music (Basse). Discussion with the children produced words such as grand, posh, processional, courtly and dignified to describe the music. The children enjoyed practising an Elizabethan processional walk and dropping their heads and bowing and curtseying when it was their turn before the monarch. The music provided the atmosphere and setting for a historical understanding about monarchy which would have been harder to reach without this particular source.

Chapter 9

Local History, Buildings and Sites, Oral History

Learning outcomes

- To gain an overview of local history for both key stages.

- To become familiar with the QCA Unit on a locality study.

- To develop an awareness of resources.

You will need

QCA Unit 11 on local history (Task 1)

A local history framework

Local history provides a wealth of opportunities through which to teach the knowledge, skills and understandings outlined in the National Curriculum document within a local framework with which children should already be familiar.

The very nature of local history means that the choice of subject matter will be heavily dependent on what has happened in the past in the area near the school and the availability of appropriate source material. Many schools cover elements of local history as an ongoing process, where it permeates work done in geography, religious education, environmental studies and English.

At some point in Key Stage 2, this is formalised into a local study unit. This gives schools three choices. They can investigate:

- how an aspect in the local area has changed over a long period of time, or

- how the locality was affected by a significant national or local event, or

- how the locality was affected by the work of a significant individual.

Many schools do more than one of these units.

It is easy to see how local history builds on topic work done at Key Stage 1 and in the Foundation Stage for the Early Learning Goals on knowledge and understanding about the world. If we are concerned with helping the very young to understand their position in time and place we will be using our knowledge of local history. Pupils and their families are an essential part of that ever-changing local history. The starting point is often the school itself, particularly when parents and even grandparents may have attended the same school.

If you are uncertain about local history, there is usually a local history section in the public library and many local authority websites contain good contact information for finding out about local history.

Tim Copeland in *Geography and the Historic Environment* (1993) provides some useful key questions. Try answering them for (i) your own area and (ii) the school locality (if different). The questions are effective in defining the very close link between locality studies in history and geography.

Key questions about a place

Present	Past	Influence of the past on the present
What is this place like?	What was this place like?	What elements of the past can we see in this place?
Why is this place as it is, how and why does it differ from or resemble other places?	Why was this place as it was, how and why did it differ from or resemble other places?	What influence have these elements had on this place, and how does this influence differ from or resemble what has happened at other places?
In what ways is this place connected with other places?	In what ways was this place connected with other places?	In what ways have past connections influenced how this place is now connected with other places?
How is this place changing and why?	How did this place change and why?	How did this place change and why and how are those changes reflected in the present?
What would it feel like to be in this place?	What would it have felt like to be in this place?	How does the past influence what it feels like to be in this place?

The QCA Unit on local history (Unit 11) links locality studies with the Victorians. Many schools have chosen to do this or to link with another relevant study (e.g. Romans in Chester, Vikings in York). The QCA Unit is aimed at the top end of KS2 and requires children to compare one period in the past (1841) with another (1891). Younger pupils and children at the Foundation Stage are more likely to look at concrete evidence of the Victorian era in the buildings around them and photographs taken of the local area in the late Victorian period. They see it as 'Then' as compared to 'Now'. 100 years ago is another way of looking at it, so that time past appears in a manageable chunk.

Older pupils need access to many of the historical sources we have covered already in this guide – artefacts, visual sources and written sources. A well organised local history study gives them access to the originals. All children need access to other sources which will be covered later in this unit – buildings, sites and oral history.

 Down load Unit 11 from the relevant QCA website (www.open.gov.uk/qca/). Read through the five questions posed in Unit 11 and try answering them to see how much you know about your local area in Victorian times.

Who lived here in 1841?

Who lived and worked here in 1891? What changed since 1841 and why?

How did the arrival and expansion of the railways affect our area?

What evidence of Victorian times remains in our area?

How did life change in our locality in Victorian times?

You may want to do this for another historical period, such as Britain since 1930; the Roman/Anglo-Saxon/Viking period; the Tudors.

The historic environment

Copeland's booklet (1993) explores the historical and geographical potential of individual sites and local landscapes. Its main historical focus is on activities that children can undertake when they explore the local landscape or visit an historic monument or site.

This involves showing:

- how the present landscape is a product of the past
- how to look at individual historic components of the landscape to see how they survive today and how they functioned in the past
- the importance of considering the needs of historic places today and some of the tensions that can arise between these needs.

Copeland then looks at sources such as maps, plans, aerial photographs, sites and monuments. He later classifies different sites thus:

- defensive – hill forts, Roman forts, castles and pillboxes
- ceremonial and religious – prehistoric ceremonial sites, churches, abbeys
- industrial – prehistoric sites, sites of the industrial revolution
- settlement sites – villages, towns.

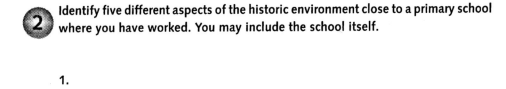 **Identify five different aspects of the historic environment close to a primary school where you have worked. You may include the school itself.**

1.

2.

3.

4.

5.

What additional resources could be used inside school to provide additional primary source material for any one of these aspects? When you have read through the rest of this section on local history resources, return to this question and identify what else you may need to do in order to increase your own subject knowledge.

Local history resources*

Current and historical maps can provide useful source material for finding out about the past in a particular locality. If you are going back to the Tudor period, Speed's maps of different counties are beautiful historical sources. Each map has a 3-D inset of the county town, which gives a lovely visual source for the structure of Tudor townships. On a more local level, maps from this period often provide an interesting insight into local industries and ways in which people were punished, such as ducking stools, whipping posts and stocks! This makes the more distant past come alive, especially if you see a map showing a ducking stool about five minutes from your house.

Local libraries, record offices and planning departments are also useful starting points for maps and resources. Local history books aimed at the adult market often contain maps which can be adapted for young children. In school you need to have several copies of different types of maps for children to work on. Try to ensure that the geographical skills needed for interpreting maps are matched with work on mapping being undertaken in geography.

1. **School plans** – now and then. Even quite new school buildings often have had extensions and conversions. Work was done on a nursery plan with under fives when the nursery was extended and the children compared the two plans with their existing nursery.

2. **Street scenes** – tourist maps in particular show how buildings may have changed their use; for example Chester Castle is now used as a military museum, and other streets have religious names such as Nun's Road and Trinity Street. This shows the ecclesiastical history of the city. Many towns and cities have trade streets – Weaver Street, Pottery Fields and so on.

3. **Ordnance Survey** maps show ancient tracks and remains.

4. **Place names on regional or national maps** – looking for evidence of Roman, Anglo-Saxon and Viking settlement. More able readers can use adult place name dictionaries to help them track down the origins of local place names.

5. **Changing cities** – a series of maps of the nearest local city/large town over a period of time. As well as showing the growth of a city they can also reveal street names that stay the same, those which change and streets which disappear altogether. Victorian growth is particularly interesting to see from local city maps and this helps children to identify some of the many problems which came with the movement of people from the country to the city.

6. **Growth of the seaside** – there are some lovely Victorian maps of towns such as Blackpool and Brighton, which show how the railways made it possible for people to get out of the towns to visit seaside resorts. Maps of Blackpool taken from 1844 and 1897, for example, show evidence of additional house building, three piers, a lifeboat station, Blackpool tower and railway lines and station. Older KS2 pupils can begin to discuss how towns and cities like this grew, where the cheaper accommodation was likely to be situated and ways in which tourism became a major industry.

7. **Tithe maps** – these maps were made by the parish to show how much land different individuals owned and included details such as ponds, the types of fields and other land. One tenth (a tithe) of the annual produce of the land or labour was taken by the church as a tax. Tithe barns were built to store the tithes which were paid in kind. It is worth searching for tithe maps for the school locality. Like the inventories, they open up a very intimate part of the past and, with good teaching, make it come alive.

---

*Ideas for this section are taken from Hughes, P. (1997) *Local History*.

QCA Scheme of Work

'Update 2000' added an additional unit for local history entitled What was it like to live here in the past? (QCA 2000). This focuses on encouraging an enquiry-based approach to a local history study. The emphasis is on use of written and oral sources to find out about the past. It suggests using census returns, trade directories, school records and inventories. Children should be encouraged to present their findings in a variety of different ways – wall or table display, guide book, tape/slide show, oral presentation, drama or a timeline. The cynic might wonder whether the ICT element of the history update was written by the same person as this unit, since ICT is thrown in simply as a way in which children could sort information. The more imaginative uses of ICT in presentation, e.g. the creation of a local history school website or powerpoint presentation, seem to be absent.

The changing landscape

Let children look at the landscape around the school and suggest ways in which it may have changed over the years. Simple changes in people's lives can influence the landscape, for example the growth of early settlements and changes in farming methods. More recently, changes in working patterns, leisure, entertainment, transport and shopping have all influenced the landscape. Discussion here often links closely to geography. Landscape changes are not always welcomed and often fought against, for example increased traffic on roads, changes in the skyline caused by 'attractions' such as the Millennium Dome, retail centres, car and coach parks, litter and pollution. There are very clear PSHE issues here as well as citizenship themes and it is important that history is seen as a dynamic force, where evidence is sought, evaluated and presented as accurately as possible.

Place names

Many place names have grown over time, so that an Anglo-Saxon word may have been added to a Celtic word to create a placename. The Scandinavian invasion and settlement which took place during the 9th, 10th, and 11th centuries resulted in many placenames of Scandinavian origin in the north and east of England. By the time the Normans arrived most settlements and landscape features already had established names. French names were given to the newly built castles, estates and monasteries – Battle and Belvoir, for example. French-speaking families often added their names to their manors. This resulted in many double-barrelled names, for example Sutton Courtenay, Stanton Lacy.

More generally, place names can be divided into three main groups – folk names, habitative names and topographical names. Folk names are derived from the original inhabitants of the area. Essex and Sussex are both old Anglo-Saxon kingdoms for example. Habitative names show places which have been inhabited from very early times. So the place name describes a particular kind of habitation, for example homesteads, farms, enclosures, villages, cottages and other kinds of buildings and settlements. Topographical names originally consisted of a description of some topographical or physical feature – natural or made by humans. This name was then transferred to any settlement near the landscape feature named. The names for rivers, streams, fords, roads, marshes and moors, hills and valleys are often found in place names.

1. **Collecting words** – encourage children to look at the environmental print around them to find clues about the past, such as street names, historic signs (shops, pubs, bi-lingual signs).

2. **Celtic, Roman, Anglo-Saxon, Viking and Norman** – can children find evidence of suffixes and prefixes which indicate the origin of a local place name? Hughes (1997) provides a comprehensive review of the most common of these.

Archaeological remains

Archaeology is all about building up a picture of how people lived in the past from the clues that they left behind. Encourage children to develop their skills of interpretation through working systematically on local artefacts which will involve them in observations, recording and analysis.

Movable remains, such as coins and jewellery. These are often found in local museums, although sadly many good local finds end up in the British Museum. Lindow Man found just outside Manchester is now tucked away in a corner of the British Museum. When it was shown in Manchester, two of the authors visited and saw a beautiful, evocative and imaginative display taking up a whole room. This essentially spiritual element of the Celtic culture is completely lost in the British Museum exhibit. It also loses local remains for local study. However, there are still good local collections which children can visit.

Interpreting remains – Local collections are often controversial. The local history aspect is less so, but many local museums also contain items from wider archaeological collections held locally. These may include Egyptian mummies, Roman statues, Greek pots and African masks collected over a period of time, often through the 'Grand Tours' favoured by local gentry from the 16th century onwards. These bring a very local view to the ways in which museums hold objects which have been stolen or taken from other countries.

Class museums – Requests for local artefacts often bring surprising results. Children can be encouraged to look at local artefacts in ways used by archaeologists. They start by creating a database which describes and suggests possible uses for the object and then move on to look at other sources of information, such as non-fiction texts which can provide printable dates.

Buildings

These are the most obvious remains in any locality for children to observe and analyse. Children at the Foundation Stage and at KS1 start with the school itself. They need to learn to classify different aspects of buildings in their locality. This can be easily graded for different age groups, but by the end of their primary education children should be able to identify:

- **different types of building materials,** such as stone and brick work, and relate this to different types of construction in their own area.

- **roofing differences** – materials such as thatch, slate, tile; the presence and absence of chimney pots.

- **doors and windows** – the different types to be found in the neighbourhood. If there is a rich variety of doors/windows from different periods children can use observational drawings to make a timeline for their own area.

- **local architectural features** – pupils need a vocabulary for this which will vary with local circumstances. Words might include lintel, cornice, pediment, fanlight, sash windows, plinth, pillar and gallery.

- **historical borrowing** – in many cities, architects borrowed from ancient civilisations for their buildings. The ancient Greeks borrowed from the Egyptians and many major cities have used Greek columns and Islamic domes to enhance the appearance of their public buildings. Children can identify these borrowings and discuss when these buildings were constructed. Architects for local housing estates may have borrowed from the past as well, for example Tudor frontages. Children can discuss the differences between the original houses and the 1990's version, in which they may be living.

- **pollution and local history** – towns and cities which grew up during the industrial revolution are good examples of how town development took place in the interests of factory owners. They built their own houses away from the pollution created by their factories, while their workers lived and worked close to the factory. Children can discuss how their town has changed from this pattern and developed.

- **places of safety and defence** – children living close to a walled city, fort, dyke, castle or pillbox could investigate why their area needed such a defence.

- **houses** – even very young children can investigate changes in their own homes – an extension for a new baby, a living/dining room knocked into one. Even very new housing has often been changed from its original design and children may remember ways in which the structure of their house has been altered since they moved in.

- **changing houses** – let children look at housing in their own locality, identify houses that were built at different times and make a simple timeline of local housing. Make sure that children living in older property are not made to feel that this is any way inferior to living in a much newer house. Children can be asked to look at houses near the school and find three built at different times. These could be sketched and made into a local housing timeline.

- **stately homes** – visits can show how people lived in the past and the different types of lifestyles which went on in the same house, for example 'upstairs' and 'downstairs'. The gardens and grounds of stately homes are often more accessible for young children and give them an opportunity of looking at the exterior of houses and different ways in which gardens were kept. Herb gardens are particularly interesting because they throw a light on the treatment of illness in the past. Durbin and Hollingshead's *A Teachers' Guide to Using Historic Houses* (1993) in the English Heritage Education on Site series provides good support for visits to all sorts of houses, including empty and ruined ones.

There is a secondary bias to this, but ideas can be adapted and used for both Key Stage 1 and 2. Eric Maddern (1992) suggests a rationale and history for storytelling in *A Teacher's Guide to Storytelling at Historic Sites* in the same series.

- **schools** – children can look at ways in which their school building has changed over the years. Encourage them to suggest reasons why it has changed. A checklist helps to provide a structured response to changes both inside and outside the building. As discussed in Chapter 6, Written Sources, there are plenty of additional resources which can be used for a local history topic on 'Our School', such as logbooks, punishment books, minutes and newspaper cuttings. Purkis (1993) gives good support to the use of the school as an historic site and provides clear guidance to ways in which progression can be shown throughout the primary school.

The ideas below originally appeared in an article by Pat Hughes in *Child Education*, (November 1992).

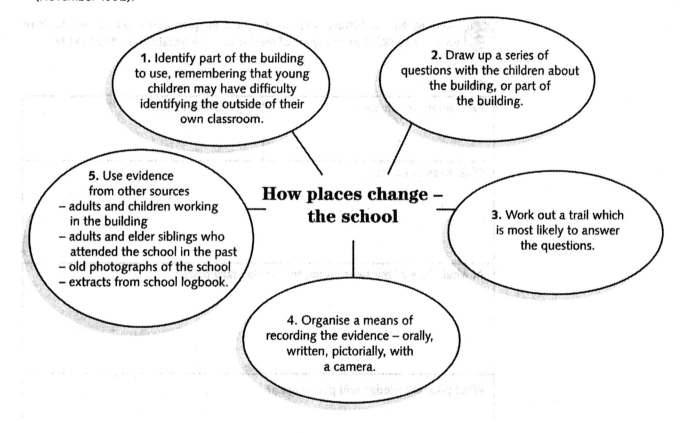

Monuments – remembering and worship

Encourage the children to take note of the ways in which the local community has commemorated courage and achievement, and how the people celebrate their faith and beliefs, by observing and exploring:

- plaques and dates on the inside and outside of buildings

- memorials – war memorials, gifts to the local community in the name of someone (strained glass windows, extension to buildings and so on). Purkis (1995) can be used to support this aspect of local history

- places of worship – identifying different types and faiths in the local community, knowing names for different parts of the building and the associated beliefs. There are links with RE here.

Oral history

Oral history means spoken accounts of events and experiences and covers both the past and present. Local museums and history societies may keep taped recordings and supplement these with photographs and written records. You as the teacher are probably the most useful oral history resource for children at both key stages and there will be other people within the school who can provide initial models for systematic recording of local history.

 Planning an oral history session: complete the plan below, based on a topic of your choice (KS1) or an aspect of the history unit Britain since 1930 (KS2)

Topic:

Who would you invite?	Type of oral history
Objectives of session:	
At what stage of the topic would the session take place?	
What prior knowledge will pupils need?	
What historical source would support the session?	

Allan Redfern in Chapter 4 of *History and English in the Primary School* (Hoodless 1998) gives an excellent rationale and overview of oral history in the primary curriculum. He discusses the nature of oral history activity and then looks at practical teaching strategies, i.e.

- ensuring children understand the purpose of what they are doing
- teaching them to use tape recorders and video cameras
- identifying appropriate respondents
- preparing questions
- conducting interviews
- analysing, summarising, editing and transcribing using oral testimony.

He goes on to link this with the history key elements and Programmes of Study at both key stages and demonstrates his points with two case studies.

Parental involvement in local history outside school

Parents and carers can play an important role in fostering the development of children's historical understanding and skills, and teachers should actively seek their involvement in the following areas:

1. *Talking and listening*
- exploring historical vocabulary (yesterday, long ago, last week)
- discussing family relationships
- telling stories about their own childhood and their child's

2. *Reading and telling stories*
- about the past
- myths and legends
- picture books showing illustrations about the past

3. *Collecting historical data*
- photographs and artefacts about the child's own history
- the historical perspectives of existing collections of photographs, stamps, coins, football programmes

4. *Making time*
- time to listen, time to talk, time to share

5. *Organising visits involving travel*
- historical buildings and sites

- specialist museums and heritage sites

- stately homes

- places of worship

6. *Encouraging local involvement*
- looking at buildings and sites in the area

- observing street names for clues about the area in the past

- joining and using the local library

- visiting local museums and places of interest

- going to places of worship

- sequencing regular journeys to school, the park, shops, visiting relatives

- discussing irregular visits, such as holidays.

Bibliography and References

Ahlberg, A. and Ahlberg, J. (1983) *Peepo*, Picture Puffins.

Airs, J. and Ball, C. (1995) *Drama*, Folens.

Andreetti, K. (1993) *Teaching History from Primary Evidence*, David Fulton Publishers.

Beardsley, G. (1998) *Exploring Play in the Primary Classroom*, David Fulton Publishers (chapter on exploring history through play).

Blyth, J. (1994) *History 5 to 11*, Hodder and Stoughton.

Blyth, J. and Hughes, P. (1997) *Using Written Sources in Primary History*, Hodder and Stoughton.

Bradman, T. and Dupasquier, P. (1990) *The Sandal*, Puffin.

Brighton, C. (2000) *Mozart*, Francis Lincoln.

Claire, H. (1996) *Reclaiming Our Pasts*, Trentham Books.

Clipson-Boyles, S. (1998) *Drama in Primary English Teaching*, David Fulton Publishers.

Cooper, H. (1995) *History in the Early Years*, Routledge.

Cooper, H. (2000) *The Teaching of History in the Primary School: Implementing the Revised National Curriculum*, 3rd edn, David Fulton Publishers.

Copeland, T. (1993) *Geography and the Historic Environment*, English Heritage.

Cox, K. and Hughes, P. (1990) *Starting History Photopacks*, Scholastic.

Cox, K., Goddard, G. and Hughes, P. (2000) *Primary Foundations History 7–11*, Scholastic.

Croll, P. and Hastings, N. (1996) *Effective Primary Teaching*, David Fulton Publishers.

Davies, I. and Webb, C. (1986) *Using Documents*, English Heritage.

DES (1990) *National Curriculum, History Working Group – Final Report*, DES.

DfEE/QCA (1998a) *A Scheme of Work for History, Update 2000*, DfEE/QCA.

DfEE (1998b) *A Scheme of Work for Key Stages 1 and 2: History*, DfEE/QCA.

DfEE (1998c) *The National Literacy Strategy, Module 6: Reading and Writing for Information*, DfEE.

DfEE/QCA (1999a) *Early Learning Goals*, DfEE/QCA.

DfEE/QCA (1999b) *The National Curriculum 1999*, DfEE/QCA.

DfEE/QCA (1999c) *The National Curriculum Handbook for Primary Teachers in England*, DfEE/QCA.

Durbin, G. *et al.* (1990) *A Teacher's Guide to Learning from Objects*, English Heritage.

Durbin, G. and Hollingshead, L. (1993) *A Teacher's Guide to Using Historic Houses*, English Heritage.

First Steps (1997) *Reading Resource Book*, Rigby Heinemann.

Handford, M. (1990) *Where's Wally?* Walker Books.

Historical Association (1997) *School Museums and Primary History*, Occasional Paper, The Historical Association.

HMI (1985) *History in the Primary and Secondary Years*, HMSO.

Hoodless, P. (1996) *Time and Timelines in the Primary School*, Historical Association.

Hoodless, P. (1998) *History and English in the Primary School: Exploiting the Links*, Routledge.

Hughes, P. (1993) *Teaching History*, Oxford University Press.

Hughes, P. (1997) *Local History*, Scholastic.

Hughes, P. (1998) 'Visual Literacy' in Evans, J. (ed.) *Whats in the Picture?* Paul Chapman.

Keith, C. (1991) *Using Listed Buildings*, English Heritage.

Lewis, M. and Wray, D. (1995) *Developing Children's Non-fiction Writing: working with writing frames*, Scholastic.

Lomas, T. (1990) *Teaching and Assessing Historical Understanding,* The Historical Association.

Lomas, T. *et al.* (1996) *Planning Primary History for the Revised National Curriculum*, Murray.

Lynn, S. (1993) 'Children Reading Pictures: History Visuals at Key Stages 1 and 2', *Education 3-13*, **21***(3) 23–30.*

Maddern, E. (1992) *A Teacher's Guide to Storytelling at Historic Sites*, English Heritage.

Mallett, M. (1992) *Making Facts Matter*, Paul Chapman.

Morris, S. (1989) *A Teacher's Guide to Using Portraits*, English Heritage.

Neate, B. (1999) *Finding Out About Finding Out*, Hodder and Stoughton.

Purkis, S. (1993) *Using School Buildings*, English Heritage.

Purkis, S. (1995) *Using Memorials*, English Heritage.

QCA (1999) *Speaking and Listening*, QCA.

QCA (2000) *History Teachers' Guide Update*, QCA/DfEE.

Redfern, A. (1998) 'Voices of the Past', in Hoodless, P. *History and English in the Primary School*, Routledge.

Redfern, A. (1998) 'Living with the National Curriculum', *Oral History: Journal of the Oral History Society*, **26** *(1).*

SCAA (1997) *History and the Use of Language: Key Stages 1 & 2*, SCAA.

Smart, J. (1994) *The Past Speaks Out: Exploring your environment through historical investigation.*

Trussell-Cullen, A. (1989) *A Pocket Full of Posies! A History of Nursery Rhymes*, Literacy Links.

Further Sources of Information

English Heritage

In addition to the publications listed in the Bibliography and References section, the Education Service at English Heritage has an extensive range of handbooks for teachers and videos for curriculum use both by pupils and teachers. Videos can be borrowed by teachers on free loan.
English Heritage, Education Service, 429 Oxford Street, London W1R 2HD. Tel: 020 7973 3442.
www. english-heritage.org.uk

The National Trust

The website of the National Trust has notes for teachers and information that pupils can use for research. It covers country houses and more general conservation projects.
www.nationaltrust.org.uk/education

Television

1. BBC Landmarks: A cross-curricular programme with blocks of geography and history, aimed officially at 9- to 12-year-olds. Often these programmes rely on giving information rather than on reconstruction.

2. BBC Zig-Zag: This also has blocks of geography and history but is aimed at the younger age group of seven- to nine-year-olds.

3. BBC Watch: Although designed for KS1, it might be of use at Y3.

4. C4 Eureka: This is aimed at 7- to 11-year-olds and provides a cross-curricular approach, such as history through art.

5. C4 How We Used to Live: Now aimed at 7- to 11-year-olds, this principally uses drama reconstructions, which is very successful as a formula.

6. The 'Magic Grandad' series and the 'Famous People' series work well.

Websites

Some other useful websites are:

www.24hourmuseum.org.uk
> General information about local museums and English Heritage sites

www.akhet.freeserve.co.uk/cairo.htm
> The Cairo Museum

www.british-museum.ac.uk/
> The British Museum

www.genealogy.bookpub.net
> Trace your ancestors

www.hope.ac.uk/index.htm
> Details of additional history articles by the three authors of this guide

www.learnfree.co.uk
> Starting point or finding history sites

www.nc.uk.net
> The National Curriculum

www.nationalgallery.org.uk/collection/content.htm
> The National Gallery

www.npg.org.uk/search
www.npg.org.uk/roomsg.htm
> The National Portrait Gallery

www.open.gov.uk/qca
> The Qualifications and Curriculum Authority (QCA)

www.thehistorychannel.co.uk/
> TV history channel

See also Chapter 7, section on History and the Web.

Index